The Secret That Murder, Inc. *WANTED* Abe Reles To Spill!

...USE ABE SANG...

Kid Twist warbled plenty to the D.A., but the "boys" wished he'd added one more chorus before his swan song...

THE Canary Sang BUT Couldn't Fly

THE Canary Sang BUT Couldn't Fly

The Fatal Fall of Abe Reles,
the Mobster Who Shattered
Murder, Inc.'s Code of Silence

EDMUND ELMALEH

UNION SQUARE PRESS
An imprint of Sterling Publishing Co., Inc.

New York / London
www.sterlingpublishing.com

STERLING and the distinctive Sterling logo are
registered trademarks of Sterling Publishing Co., Inc.

Library of Congress Cataloging-in-Publication Data

Elmaleh, Edmund.
The canary sang but couldn't fly: the fatal fall of Abe Reles, the mobster
who shattered Murder, Inc.'s code of silence / by Edmund Elmaleh.
p. cm.
Includes bibliographical references and index.
ISBN 978-1-4027-6113-3
1. Reles, Abe, 1906-1941. 2. Criminals--United States--Biography.
3. Mafia--United States--History--20th century. I. Title.
HV6446.E45 2009
364.1092--dc22
[B]
2008041353

2 4 6 8 10 9 7 5 3 1

Published by Sterling Publishing Co., Inc.
387 Park Avenue South, New York, NY 10016
© 2009 by Edmund Elmaleh
Map of Brooklyn © 2009 by Alan Kikuchi
Distributed in Canada by Sterling Publishing
^c⁄o Canadian Manda Group, 165 Dufferin Street
Toronto, Ontario, Canada M6K 3H6
Distributed in the United Kingdom by GMC Distribution Services
Castle Place, 166 High Street, Lewes, East Sussex, England BN7 1XU
Distributed in Australia by Capricorn Link (Australia) Pty. Ltd.
P.O. Box 704, Windsor, NSW 2756, Australia

Sterling ISBN 978-1-4027-6113-3

For information about custom editions, special sales, premium and
corporate purchases, please contact Sterling Special Sales
Department at 800-805-5489 or specialsales@sterlingpublishing.com.

For Kathi Kapell, who means everything to me

and

in loving memory of Elaine, Lorraine, and Eliott

"Never rat on your friends, and always keep your mouth shut."
— *A mobster's advice to his young protégé,*
from the movie Goodfellas

"You don't know those bastards like I do.
Anywhere in the world they'd find me, if I was on the outside.
Anywhere in the world—and they'd knock me off!"
— *Abe Reles on the Mob's determination to assassinate him*

"I never met anybody who thought Abe went out
that window because he wanted to."
— *Mob informer Joe Valachi on Reles's death*

3 miles

MANHATTAN

QUEENS

Hudson River

East River

Williamsburg

Albert Anastasia's Territory

Ocean Hill

Sunrise Garage

Red Hook

Midnight Rose's

Residential Courtyard

East New York

UPPER NEW YORK BAY

Brownsville

Abe Reles's Home

BROOKLYN

Morris Diamond's Murder

JAMAICA BAY

GRAVESEND BAY

Coney Island

Half Moon Hotel

ATLANTIC OCEAN

N W E S

KEY

Abe Reles's Home Site of Irving Feinstein's murder, September 4, 1939
Albert Anastasia's Territory The docks and beyond
Half Moon Hotel Site of Abe Reles's death, November 12, 1941
Midnight Rose's Site of Combination's headquarters
Morris Diamond's Murder In a street intersection, May 25, 1939
Residential Courtyard Site of Alex Alpert's murder, November 25, 1933
Sunrise Garage Site of George Rudnick's murder, May 25, 1937

Contents

List of Illustrations

Prologue

Wednesday, November 12, 1941
Coney Island, Brooklyn, New York

It's 4:30 a.m. and four men are lounging around in the lobby of Coney Island's Half Moon Hotel. George Govans, the night bellhop, is stretched out on a sofa, griping about the Brooklyn Dodgers with Charles Burns and Thomas Doyle, two New York City cops who are on assignment at the hotel. The three men still can't believe that "Dem Bums" (as Brooklynites called the Dodgers) had won their first pennant in twenty-one years—only to be trounced by the hated Yankees in the recent World Series.

A few feet away, Alfred Wolfarth, the hotel's building engineer, is dozing off in a chair after laboring for hours in the boiler room.

Suddenly a loud thud coming from the east side of the building reverberates through the lobby.

Wolfarth is jolted awake. "What was that?" he cries out.

"Sounds like someone ran into the wall," Govans says, convinced that a car has jumped a curb in the parking lot and bumped into the hotel.

Since neither of the cops seems in any hurry to investigate, Wolfarth and Govans are tempted to do a bit of sleuthing. But it's cold, windy, and pitch-black outside, so they decide to wait until daylight. By then, however, they've forgotten about the incident.

At 7:00 a.m., William Nicholson, chief clerk of the Coney Island draft board, enters his office in room 123 of the Half Moon Hotel. Something outside the window catches his eye. His heart skips a beat when he sees the motionless body of a man lying facedown a few feet away on the kitchen extension roof. His hands trembling, Nicholson phones Alexander Lysberg, the hotel's assistant manager. "Something's happened," he says, struggling to stay calm.

"What is it?" Lysberg asks.

"I can't tell you over the phone," Nicholson responds.

Lysberg hurries from his room on the eleventh floor down to the draft board office. He finds Nicholson, pale as a ghost, pointing to the window.

"Look out there," Nicholson says.

When Lysberg peers out, he can't believe his eyes: It's Abe Reles.

Lysberg rushes into the street and notifies Patrolmen Burns and Doyle (who have returned to their posts guarding the entrances to the building) about the body. The trio hurries to the extension roof. They find Abe Reles lying on his stomach, his left arm flung out, the left side of his face pockmarked with gravel from the roof. He's wearing a gray suit, white shirt, blue sweater, and black shoes. Two bedsheets, tied together, are fluttering near the body; a strip of insulated wire is tied to the end of one of the sheets. Burns dashes into the draft board office, where he calls his station house and tells the police dispatcher to send radio cars and an ambulance to the hotel right away.

The dispatcher who gets Burns's urgent message tries to remain calm. He wants to avoid attracting the attention of the pack of police reporters who are breathing down his neck, hoping to pick up a hot tip on a breaking story. But the reporters, with their press cards tucked into the hatbands of their rumpled fedoras, have a sixth sense about this sort of thing. *Something's up,* they mutter to one another. *Something big.*

Back at the Half Moon, Lysberg phones hotel manager Paul Fulton with the shocking news. Fulton in turn dials up to a suite on the sixth floor; Detective Victor Robbins of the NYPD, on assignment at the hotel, answers.

"Abe is out the window!" Robbins yells to the four other cops in the suite after Fulton breaks the news to him. He drops the phone, draws his gun, and dashes down the hall and into Reles's room. A portable radio is playing, but Reles is gone. Hoping against hope that the man lying on the extension roof isn't Reles, Robbins anxiously approaches the large, wide-open window and gazes down. The scene fifty-two feet below hits him like a nightstick in the gut.

His heart pounding wildly, Detective Robbins phones his boss, Police Captain Frank Bals. "Abe is out the window," he tells Bals, trying to avoid saying too much on a phone that may be tapped.

"How did he get out?" the captain demands, biting back his anger.

"I don't know," Robbins answers meekly.

Bals slams down the phone. He must get to the scene on the double, but first he has to make a call that he absolutely dreads. He dials up Brooklyn district attorney William O'Dwyer, his boss and longtime friend, and relates the news that Reles has apparently fallen from his window. Bals braces for a fierce dressing-down, but the DA simply tells him to get to the bottom of what's happened. O'Dwyer's cool reaction is the last thing Bals expected.

At about 7:30 a.m., Dr. Max Silberman of nearby Coney Island Hospital arrives at the scene. He places his stethoscope against Reles's chest, but there is only silence. He checks for a pulse, but there is none. "It's a DOA," he says matter-of-factly.

As Dr. Silberman is preparing to leave, a uniformed cop pulls him aside and, in a low, menacing tone, warns him not to discuss what he has seen with anyone.

PART I

MURDER
WAS HIS
BUSINESS

Chapter 1

Kid Twist and the Combination

Abe Reles was a living, breathing, nightmare.

Just the look in his eyes was enough to fill anyone with fear.

"His eyes were shiny agates, hard and piercing," recalled Burton Turkus, an assistant district attorney who came to know him well. "He had a round face, thick lips, a flat nose, and small ears stuck close to his kinky hair." His jowls were heavy, his five o'clock shadow ever present, his voice gravelly from chain-smoking. His hirsute arms "dangled to his knees, completing a generally gorilla-like figure." Even if you could get past his unsightly mug, there was one thing that you could never put out of your mind: his hands.

"They were strong; they strangled men," Turkus remembered. "Where ordinary fingers start to taper at the ends, Reles's became spatulate. They reminded you of a set of hammers, hung at the end of the arm."

As far as Turkus was concerned, you didn't even have to know Abe Reles to loathe him. "If a total stranger walked up to Reles and, without a word, bashed him in the face, I could understand it. That was the reaction you got from one look at him."

Not that anybody in his right mind would have tried. While not physically imposing—he wasn't a big man at five foot five and 160 pounds—Reles was tough, menacing, and extremely violent. A stone-cold killer, he once strangled a man to death as his own mother-in-law slept just a few feet away. (He did, however, wake the elderly woman long enough to ask where he could find the rope he needed to choke the life out of his victim.) During his criminal career, which began when Reles was only a teenager, he was arrested more than forty times, including six times on murder charges. But each homicide rap was thrown out due to "lack of evidence," a sign that Reles had greased the palm of some crooked judge. If he found himself short of cash for bribes, Reles had an effective Plan B: threatening or killing the witnesses against him.

Reles had a volcanic temper, and he was capable of unimaginable brutality. A police officer who knew him well recalled the time that he "tore the head off a kitten right in his own living room by sheer force with his fingers. The kitten had climbed on the settee and he didn't like it, and he took the kitten and tore the head off and threw it out." Another time, Reles grew impatient with a garage attendant who was working too slowly to suit him—so he smashed a bottle over the young man's head, fracturing his skull. Once, when two young women spurned his lewd advances, he jumped into his car and tried to run them over; the women survived by ducking into an alley at the last second. Yes, Abe Reles was a real prince.

As a young man, he revered Max Zweibach, a lieutenant in the Lower East Side gang of Monk Eastman. In 1904, when Eastman went to prison for shooting at a Pinkerton detective during a bank holdup, Zweibach seized control of the gang. His intricate schemes for outsmarting his rivals earned him the moniker Kid Twist. Zweibach led the gangster life until May 1908, when he and his bodyguard, a circus strongman known as Cyclone Lewis, were gunned down outside a Coney Island bar. The killer, Louis "Louie the Lump" Pioggi, allegedly acted out of jealousy—he and Zweibach were in love with the same woman—but Pioggi's membership in a rival gang suggests that the murder may not have been entirely a crime of passion.

Abe "Kid Twist" Reles. [Corbis]

Reles adopted Zweibach's nickname, Kid Twist, as his own. (Contrary to much that has been written, Reles was not given the nickname because of a fondness for licorice twist candy or a preference for strangling his victims.) Though Reles now had Zweibach's nickname, he did not possess an ounce of his idol's finesse; rather, he was egotistical, crude, and miserly. With an inflated view of himself, Reles believed that he could outwit cops, lawyers, judges—you name it. But his loud attire and coarse speech (which was littered with *dese* and *dose*) made a joke out of any stabs he made at appearing suave. And his penny-pinching was legendary among his cadre of crooks.

"He was reluctant to pay and made no bones about it," one of them remembered. Reles enjoyed forcing his compatriots to pony up for everything while he flashed large wads of cash under their noses. It's safe to say that even those closest to Reles hated his guts.

■■■

The future menace to society was born in Manhattan on May 10, 1906, to Sam Reles and Rose Schulman, Jewish immigrants from Austria. Of the nearly two million Jews who migrated to the United States from Eastern Europe during the final decade of the nineteenth century and the first two decades of the twentieth, most settled in the foul, claustrophobic tenements of Manhattan's Lower East Side. The Reles family's experience was no different. It was a far cry from the Golden Land (*Die Goldene Medina*, as it is expressed in Yiddish) the immigrants had envisioned as they crossed the ocean in the bowels of transatlantic liners. Once on American soil, any hopeful thoughts they still held dear were snuffed out by the realities of life. Winter forced families to sleep on the floor to absorb the warmth of their ramshackle kitchen stoves; the most basic privacy was nonexistent, and infectious diseases stole lives indiscriminately. Work, such as it existed, was a dismal euphemism for grinding poverty. It was enough to drive Sam Reles to distraction.

And then, a glimmer of hope. The opening of the Williamsburg Bridge—which connected Manhattan with Brooklyn in 1903—as well as other advances in public transportation "came in time to relieve the Lower East Side." As a result, Brownsville, a community in northeast

Brooklyn, "became for large numbers their new home in the Golden Land." What's more, as the Brooklyn historian Alter F. Landesman has written, the rapid rise of Brownsville was not due to the discovery of any one commodity, as was the case in boomtowns elsewhere in America. In Brownsville, "tailors were the original pioneers; sewing machines, flat irons, scissors, needles, and thimbles—these were the foundation materials upon which the community was built."

Tailors! It seemed too good to be true. Sam Reles was a tailor; he'd learned his trade back in the Old Country. It seemed like a sign from above. Soon after Abe's birth, Sam moved the family to Brownsville. He prayed that the move would be a step up in the world, but his hopes were quickly dashed. Uncontrolled growth had undone the dream. Brownsville, as the famed journalist and social reformer Jacob Riis noted, was yet another "nasty little slum." Most of the flats, Riis observed, "are without sewers or decent drains. Families are so huddled together that even the ordinary precautions of cleanliness are next to impossible. The streets are nothing but mudholes—and where the streets are not [mired in] filth, they are deep in dust."

Brownsville did surpass Reles's old Lower East Side neighborhood in one undesirable way: "Brownsville was tougher. More guys carried guns and instead of six beatings a day there were six an hour," explained Sammy Aaronson, an amateur boxing gym operator and community activist from that era.

"Brownsville was a breeding ground of crime," wrote Aaronson, who, unlike other commentators, witnessed much of the mayhem firsthand. "Kids began a sort of spring training course for thugs when they were nine or ten years old. The insidious pattern was pretty standard. It was followed by every kid in Brownsville who went wrong. The first step was raiding penny candy and gum machines in the subway stations and corner stores. After a few months swiping pennies, the kids would start hopping wagons to steal fruits or vegetables. They would do that for a long time, maybe three years or so, before moving up to muscling pushcart peddlers, which came next."

The peddlers never stood a chance. Old and unarmed, they would be set upon by a pack of young thugs and robbed blind. After subjecting the street vendors to this frightening abuse a number of times, the punks would demand "protection" money to prevent future attacks. This enterprise yielded only small profits, "since [none of the] peddlers had enough money to live on, much less pay protection with. But it was a simple way to train for the much bigger money that was available for protection from storekeepers."

By his midteens, Aaronson explained, one of these junior crooks could "build up a reputation and pretty soon the word would get around to the big guys in New York and elsewhere that he was a 'good kid.' That meant he could be depended upon to do a job cheap and well, and a job meant anything up to and including murder."

Despite the long odds against growing up on the straight and narrow, Sammy Aaronson sincerely believed that he could have prevented Reles from pursuing a life of crime. Aaronson recalled meeting Reles when he was twelve years old. "He had a good family background," the boxing gym proprietor remembered. "His parents were nice, gentle people, but they couldn't handle the kid. They knew he was going with a tough crowd, but they were helpless to stop him." Yet Aaronson saw the signs of potential redemption: When Reles happened upon an impromptu punchball game, he shed his tough-guy persona and became just one of the boys. Reles even showed an aptitude for boxing: "Every so often he'd come around the gym and put on the gloves. He might have [become] a pretty good fighter, but he wasn't around often enough." Aaronson concluded that "tough as he became later, I don't think that Reles wanted to be a thug. A push in the right direction at the right time would have made all the difference."

In a way, it's a comforting thought: that the violence infusing Reles's life might have been avoided by something as simple as a gym where he could work out for free, and where the owner would try to give the impressionable young man a little spending money every day.

At the risk of sounding hard-hearted, Aaronson was kidding himself. Reles had long before then set his moral compass. He felt nothing but contempt for hardworking, law-abiding, God-fearing folk. Where had playing by the rules gotten them? They slaved from sunup to sundown, hawking junk in the streets or performing mind-numbing piecework in suffocating sweatshops. They came home to hovels unfit for dogs. As Reles saw it, honest work was a scam. He swore to himself that he would never be conned into doing it. No amount of punchball or sparring inside the ring would have set him right.

Ever the idealist, Aaronson pointed out that when Reles later achieved power in the Mob, he would stop by the gym and try to save the next generation by admonishing the youngsters to "do what Sammy tells you. Work hard and stay straight." Talk is cheap: Reles never once tried to straighten out any rebellious kids by sending them to Sammy for rehabilitation. Instead, he used them for his own rotten purposes: as messengers, juice loan collectors, and, in some cases, assassins. No, Abe Reles wasn't going to be asked to make any testimonials for the Boys Clubs of Brooklyn.

By age fourteen, Reles was well on his way to making good on his oath never to do an honest day's work. After dropping out of school, he notched his first run-in with the law: a 1920 theft conviction that netted him five months in juvenile hall. A felonious assault rap in 1925 sent him to the Elmira reformatory in upstate New York. Paroled in 1927, the twenty-one-year-old Reles was soon busted for armed robbery. The following year, he continued to diversify his rap sheet with arrests for burglary, robbery, and grand larceny. At the end of 1928, he violated his parole; back to Elmira he went for eighteen months. After getting out in 1930, Reles returned to Brownsville and quickly racked up two murders. The victims were street toughs who made the mistake of tangling with him. In what was to became a familiar turn of events, the judge cut him loose due to "lack of evidence."

Reles seemed destined to become just another two-bit street punk. But appearances were deceiving. After taking stock of himself, he decided not to be a bottom feeder any longer. He realized that the hustles he'd been running—stealing from pushcart peddlers, pilfering from delivery trucks, slapping around shopkeepers for a few bucks in protection money—were penny-ante crap. The serious money was in *organized* crime: loan-sharking, gambling, extortion, prostitution. When you're a big shot in those rackets, you don't just take the cash in—you *rake* it in. Finally, Reles had found some direction in his life.

He set his sights on becoming the boss of organized crime in Brownsville.

There was just one problem: The job was already taken. Meyer Shapiro, along with his brothers Irving and Willie, had been running the show for years. In a relatively short time, they'd transformed Brownsville from a wretched neighborhood into a wretched neighborhood teeming with loan sharks, extortionists, and bookmakers. The Shapiros didn't take kindly to threats to their little empire, and over the years they had made short work of all challengers. Reles knew he would need some serious muscle to take them on. In Brownsville, you could find all the muscle you needed at Label's poolroom on Sutter Avenue.

"If you wanted someone to help you break a head, beat up a guy, break a strike, buy dope, set a fire, plan a robbery, or muscle a peddler, you could find him at Label's," Sammy Aaronson declared. And what did the boys in blue do about this employment center for criminals? Not a whole hell of a lot.

"Many of the cops around Label's knew what was going on, but they never interfered," Aaronson observed. "I've seen guys dragged out of Label's screaming while a cop stood on the corner and looked the other way. I've watched a cop on the street and a hood in a car talk for twenty minutes with a victim rolled up in plain sight in the back seat, but the cop didn't ever do anything about it."

Reles recruited his first two partners at Label's: Martin "Buggsy" Goldstein and Harry "Pittsburgh Phil" Strauss. Goldstein, twenty-four, was a short, chunky hoodlum who bore a passing resemblance to tough-guy actor Edward G. Robinson. He relished playing the cutup (hence the moniker Buggsy) and always kept his fellow goons in stitches. Buggsy once wisecracked—at a police lineup, of all places—that a newspaper had ranked him sixth on its list of Brooklyn's public enemies: "I should get a better spot," he told the cops in the room. "I'm working hard on it." (He never reached the top; Reles held on to that spot from 1931 to 1940.) For all his attempts at humor, Goldstein was at heart a vicious felon. His rap sheet listed nearly thirty arrests, but only five convictions for minor offenses. He was also the chief suspect in at least ten murders.

Harry Strauss was Goldstein's polar opposite in the looks department. Tall, debonair, and vain, the twenty-one-year-old thug had a passion for fashion. It was Strauss's sartorial splendor that sparked an incident involving New York City police commissioner Lewis J. Valentine. "I remember my encounter with a manicured, elegantly dressed thug in a police lineup," Valentine recalled. "Strauss bore an easy pose in his smartly cut Chesterfield overcoat with velvet collar. His blue suit was pressed to razor sharpness and a new blue shirt held fast by a tie to match, was snug around his neck. A new pearl-gray fedora was canted over one eye at a jaunty angle." The spectacle of the impeccably attired hood was too much for Valentine. "When you meet such men draw quickly and shoot accurately," he lectured the cops in the room. "Look at him—he's the best dressed man in this room, yet he's never worked a day in his life. When you meet men like Strauss, don't be afraid to muss 'em up. Blood should be smeared all over his velvet collar."

Reles (left) and Martin "Buggsy" Goldstein laughing it up at the Brooklyn DA's office. [Brooklyn Public Library, Brooklyn Collection]

(From left) Harry "Pittsburgh Phil" Strauss,
Harry "Happy" Maione, and
Frank "The Dasher" Abbandando.
[Collections of the Library of Congress]

The remarks set off a public outcry. Was the commissioner advocating police brutality? Valentine insisted it was the furthest thing from his mind, but his clumsy efforts to deny the allegations made matters worse. Eventually the storm blew over; Valentine kept his job. And Harry Strauss kept dressing like the scion of a wealthy family.

Reles wasn't looking for fashion advice when he asked Harry to join his gang. He wanted to put to use Strauss's well-deserved reputation as a walking powder keg—"an impatient punk who would poke a fork in a waiter's eye if the restaurant service wasn't fast enough," as an acquaintance put it. Strauss, the main suspect in at least thirty murders, was "as casually cold-blooded as a meat grinding machine in a butcher shop." He considered Brownsville little more than a proving ground for his homicidal talents. "I figure I get seasoning doing these jobs here," he told a crony. "When somebody from one of the big mobs spots me, then it's up to the big leagues."

Goldstein and Strauss were itching to topple the Shapiros, but Reles knew he still needed more muscle. So he came up with a clever plan. He would convince the rival gang chief of Ocean Hill, a community adjoining Brownsville, to join him in taking on the Shapiros. The alliance would provide Reles with the extra firepower he sought *and* enable him to neutralize the Ocean Hill boys by cutting them in on the action. So he arranged for a sit-down with the gang's boss, Harry "Happy" Maione, and his deputy, Frank "Dasher" Abbandando. Maione, twenty-one, was a pint-size hood with slicked-back hair and a perpetually sour mug. (The nickname Happy was obviously someone's idea of a joke.) The twenty-year-old Abbandando was a hulking cutthroat with a wiseass smirk; he got his nickname from his days as a fleet-footed base runner for a prison baseball team.

■■■

With nicknames like "Happy" and "Dasher," these two characters might sound like a vaudeville comedy team. And while they even looked the part, with one mope towering over the other, Maione and Abbandando were anything but amusing. In addition to leaching off society, they were sexual predators. The depth of their depravity was displayed in the atrocity they perpetrated upon a young girl who was simply trying to pursue a dream.

One night, Maione, Abbandando, and two of their goons sauntered into a Brooklyn nightclub. The place was being wowed by a radiant seventeen-year-old female singer. Happy and Dasher barely heard a note of the performance; they were too busy exchanging conspiratorial glances. After the young vocalist completed her set, Abbandando approached her with a leering proposition, which she politely turned down. So the group of toughs did what came naturally. They waited until the nightclub closed, and then abducted the terrified singer when she left for home. They drove to a deserted parking lot, where the four degenerates took turns raping the defenseless young woman.

As the semiconscious victim lay at their feet, the four rapists debated whether to "bury her or buy her." After deciding on the latter, Maione and Abbandando paid a visit to the girl's mother, with whom the singer lived. After unceremoniously dumping her in the living room, they drew their guns on the mother and issued an ultimatum: "Here's $500. Keep your mouth shut, and keep the girl's mouth shut, too. Any squawks and we'll come back and get her and bury her alive."

And that was that.

■■■

Maione and Abbandando agreed to meet with Reles, Goldstein, and Strauss. But Happy and Dasher insisted that the gathering take place in their own territory. After some back-and-forth about the location, Sally's Bar and Grill on Euclid Avenue in Ocean Hill was chosen. (Everyone came armed to the teeth, just in case a double cross was in the works.) Reles came right to the point: *If youse all throw in with us, then everything we take in after clipping the Shapiros gets split right down the middle.* Maione, naturally suspicious of this sudden, generous offer, hesitated. He cast a sideways glance at Abbandando, hoping to read the thoughts of his second in command. But the dumb oaf was too busy scarfing down the sandwich he'd ordered to be bothered with any important decisions. Maione didn't really need the help. The sweet scent of easy money trumped any concerns the dyspeptic Happy may have had. Besides, if Reles tried to pull any stunts, Maione felt more than ready to take him on. *Okay, we're in,* he finally announced. There were handshakes all around as Reles and his Brownsville toughs joined forces with the Ocean Hill gang. Reles even coined a name for the new alliance: the Combination.

Reles finally had his firepower lined up, but he still wasn't good to go. Before a single trigger could be pulled, he needed to make his case for whacking the Shapiros to Umberto "Albert" Anastasia, the Mob's power broker in Brooklyn. Reles had to convince Anastasia that the Mob would profit from a regime change in Brownsville. Normally, Reles was not one to bow and scrape in search of someone else's blessing. But this was an age-old underworld custom that had to be respected. The consequences of ignoring it were sure to be lethal.

Husky, with a swarthy complexion, a bulbous nose, and dark, piercing eyes, Albert Anastasia was one of five brothers from Calabria who jumped ship in New York Harbor in 1917. Though he was then only fifteen years old, the powerfully built Anastasia quickly found employment as a longshoreman in Red Hook, the Italian section of South Brooklyn. Three of his brothers followed suit, but the fourth—clearly the black sheep of the family—eventually became a priest and returned to Italy. As fate would have it, Anastasia couldn't have picked a better time to work at the Red Hook docks. Business had taken off during World War I, continued upward in the aftermath of the conflict, and showed no signs of a downturn. The vast network of wharves and terminal buildings was constantly expanding until it occupied some five miles of the Brooklyn waterfront. And the economic impact of the Brooklyn docks was staggering: As part of the Port of New York, fully a third of the nation's foreign trade passed through this bustling commercial hub.

As the years passed, Anastasia became disenchanted with the backbreaking work of the longshoreman. (Not to mention the great danger that was a fact of life: Each time a box-and-tackle rigging swung tons of cargo overhead, Anastasia understood that the load might have his name on it.) Like Reles, Anastasia decided to move from exploited to exploiter. Almost preternaturally menacing in a line of work known for intimidating characters, Anastasia traded his work gloves and bailing hook for a lead pipe and a pistol. He followed the path laid out for him: enforcer, gunman, and, ultimately, an official in the longshoremen's union. Albert Anastasia—not yet thirty years old—was soon respected and feared as a man who didn't have to raise his voice to get things done.

Anastasia went about systematically transforming the Brooklyn waterfront into the Mob's personal grab bag. To say that he and his troops tried to steal practically everything that wasn't nailed down would be just a slight exaggeration. They pilfered on a grand scale: Crates of merchandise were pried open, and the contents handed out to the favored few.

But the plundering didn't end there. Thomas Reppetto, a longtime president of New York City's Citizens Crime Commission, asserted that the waterfront economy was tailor-made for exploitation by gangsters. First off, Reppetto noted, "the ratio of applicants to jobs was about 2 to 1. This surplus of labor meant wages could be held down and the workers kept docile. Two or three times a day men 'shaped up,' hoping to be hired as longshoremen. Hiring was the province of the dock foreman. One way to obtain the foreman's nod was for a worker to make it known that he would kick back a portion of his day's wages—20 percent was the norm." Virtually all of the four thousand men under Anastasia's control kicked back part of their paychecks to him.

Second, Reppetto argued, "Ships did not make money sitting in port. Just beyond the docks, trucks waited in crowded streets to pick up or drop off their cargo. Crews of loaders transferred cargo from the trucks to the docks. The loaders were under Mob control, and a trucker who wanted his vehicle unloaded in a timely fashion paid off." These payoffs went up the food chain and into Anastasia's pockets.

Finally, Reppetto pointed out that "the surrounding neighborhoods were crowded with dingy saloons filled with workers drinking, gambling, and whoring while they waited for the shape-up. Loan sharks were always available to advance money to men whose employment was irregular." The interest charged on the loan was, of course, astronomical. And once again, Anastasia duly received his substantial cut.

What it boiled down to was this: If you wanted anything done on the Brooklyn waterfront during Anastasia's reign, first you had to take care of Anastasia. "Albert is the head guy on the docks," Reles later said glowingly. "He is the law."

Albert Anastasia was also a dyed-in-the-wool homicidal psychopath. Dubbed "the Mad Hatter" and "the Lord High Executioner" by the press, Anastasia had a hand in approximately fifty homicides. The mere mention of his name could make even the most ferocious mobster feel uneasy. "With him it is always kill, kill, kill," recalled

Y566-3/19-NEW YORK:Albert Anastasia

Albert "The Mad Hatter" Anastasia.
[Collections of the Library of Congress]

celebrated Mob turncoat Joe Valachi. "If somebody came up and told Albert something bad about somebody else, he would say 'Hit him, hit him!'"

Time and again, Anastasia made a mockery of the judicial system. The Joe Turino rap in 1920 was a particularly galling example. Turino, a veteran long-shoreman, was considered a troublemaker who didn't fall into line as Anastasia demanded. He paid with his life for that mistake. Anastasia was convicted of whacking Turino, and was sentenced to death. A year and a half later, a new trial was granted on appeal. As the retrial date approached, the state discovered that its four key witnesses, whose testimony at the first trial doomed Anastasia, had been murdered. The state was forced to drop all charges against Anastasia, who was whisked back to Red Hook—and business as usual.

Many of Anastasia's murder victims were longshoremen who dared to challenge his authority. The case of Peter Panto is easily the most famous and, in many ways, the most poignant example. In the summer of 1939, Panto, twenty-eight, began a one-man war against Anastasia's yoke. A passionate believer in democratic principles, the charismatic young long-shoreman urged his oppressed coworkers to stand up to Mob intimidation. "We are strong," he thundered. "All we have to do is stand up and fight." Incredibly, Panto made headway: At one union meeting, close to twelve hundred of his four thousand brethren showed up to hear him declare that they must insist on honest elections in the upcoming voting for union officials. The crowd of workers, who'd seemingly thrown in the towel long ago, erupted in cheers and chants.

When reports reached Anastasia about Panto's increasing influence, the boss of the waterfront decided that the rabble-rouser had to be taken out quickly. But the situation was a touchy one. Since Panto's enemies were the mobsters and their enforcers on the waterfront, he would achieve instant martyrdom as soon as his corpse was found. It would be better for all concerned, Anastasia decreed, that Panto's body never turn up.

At ten o'clock on the night of Friday, July 14, 1939, Panto was picked up at the Brooklyn home of his fiancée by three men in a late-model car; their job was to transport him safely to a union committee meeting. His fiancée was sick with worry, but Panto promised that he'd be back in an hour. As the car sped away, the double cross went down. A huge man in the backseat shot forward and began strangling Panto while another passenger mercilessly beat him about the head and face. Panto fought for his life valiantly—he almost bit off one of the fingers of the thug who was strangling him—but he was ultimately overpowered. When Panto's body finally went limp, he was loaded into another vehicle and driven away into the night.

When Panto never returned to work, the rank-and-file longshoremen received the message loud and clear. The widespread dissent the rebel had whipped up against Anastasia evaporated.

■■■

Reles now requested a sit-down with Anastasia. Then he sat back and waited. And waited. Finally, word came down that Anastasia would see him. The meeting would be held at Anastasia's office on the Brooklyn waterfront. Reles knew that there was a chance this was a setup, and that someone—perhaps even Anastasia himself—might have tipped off the Shapiros about his plan to clip them. But the double cross was an occupational hazard, and Reles had to learn to live with it. Packing heat to the meeting wouldn't help. If Anastasia had okayed a hit, Reles was as good as dead anyway.

Fortunately for Reles, the sit-down was legitimate. Anastasia listened intently as Reles argued that the Shapiros had gotten lazy; they weren't squeezing every nickel and dime out of the rackets in

Brownsville. Why, they hadn't even collected protection fees from the new businesses popping up all over town! Impressed by Reles's fierce resolve to turn things around, and by the way he'd co-opted the Ocean Hill gang into his plans, the Mad Hatter gave his blessing to ice the Shapiros. He made it clear, however, that he wouldn't dirty his own hands in the process. It was Reles's war to win or lose. Anastasia did assign one of his top lieutenants, Louis Capone (no relation to Al), to look after his interests if the Reles faction came out on top.

Reles wasted no time in trying to liquidate the Shapiros before they could be tipped off that their days were numbered. On June 4, 1930, Meyer Shapiro and some of his henchmen were loitering outside the Globe Cafeteria on Sutter Avenue in Brownsville. Two vehicles packed with members of the Combination slowed to a crawl. In the ensuing fusillade, Meyer Shapiro was slightly wounded in the stomach, but he was able to scamper to safety. The Shapiros sent a discreet feeler through the underworld about what had happened at the Globe; word came back that they were in for the fight of their lives.

Reles flew into a rage when he learned that Meyer Shapiro had survived the attempted hit. Now, with his enemies on heightened alert, it would be that much more difficult for Reles to slay the dragon. So he plotted a different strategy. Reles reached out to a fawning neighborhood punk, Joey Silver, and instructed him to get close enough to the Shapiros to report their comings and goings.

It seemed at first that his faith in Joey Silver was well placed. Less than a week after the botched attempt, Silver passed along a tip: Meyer Shapiro, his brother and second in command, Irving, and several top lieutenants would be meeting on the evening of June 10 in an abandoned building in East New York (a Brooklyn neighborhood adjoining Brownsville). Under cover of darkness, Reles, Buggsy Goldstein, and two of Happy Maione's troops, George DeFeo and Joseph Ambrosio, slid into the pitch-dark parking lot. Suddenly the lot was crackling with gunfire. Bullets by the bushel poured out of the abandoned building. Reles was hit in the back, Buggsy Goldstein had a bit of his nose blown off, Ambrosio took a slug in his leg. DeFeo was hit in the head and died at the scene. Days later, Reles learned that the whole mess had been a double cross engineered by the treacherous Joey Silver.

In the grand tradition of the underworld, there was sure to be payback for the killing of George DeFeo. On August 27, Happy Maione spotted Joey Silver driving through Brooklyn. He tailed the traitor for several miles, and when traffic slowed he turned the wheel over to one of his deputies, leapt from the vehicle, and jumped on the running board of Silver's car. Screaming obscenities at the wide-eyed Silver, Maione jammed a .45 against Joey's chest and fired one shot directly into his heart.

The pattern of attack and counterattack continued. On September 4, Meyer Shapiro retaliated against the Combination. Samuel Cohen, one of Reles's minions, was shot and killed by a Shapiro gunman as he stood outside a small shop on Pitkin Avenue in Brownsville. The assassin then entered the store and shot two more of Reles's men; they miraculously survived the point-blank shootings.

During the winter and spring of 1930–31, the guns fell silent. Both sides in the war for Brownsville apparently went into hibernation. With the body count rising, it may have been an opportunity to recruit new blood.

The Combination came out swinging in the summer of 1931 with a major kill. Though Meyer was the Shapiro whom Reles wanted to bag first, Irving was the first to die. On July 11, 1931, Irving Shapiro attended to some business in upstate New York, then returned to Brooklyn in the evening. Reles received a tip that the brothers had met briefly and were on their way home. Licking his chops over the notion of eliminating two Shapiros in one fell swoop, he quickly gathered Maione, Abbandando, and two hit men and headed for the Shapiro family residence at 691 Blake Avenue. But Meyer Shapiro had a change of plans and decided to go to a Turkish bath before calling it a day. His weary brother begged off and headed home, where Reles and his crew were waiting. Before Irving Shapiro had a chance to wonder why the vestibule of the building was completely dark (Reles had unscrewed the single lightbulb), eighteen slugs ripped him apart.

Brownsville began to resemble Dodge City more and more with each passing day. In the wee hours of July 19, Reles was tipped off that

Meyer Shapiro had been seen wandering down a dimly lit street. Reles, Strauss, and Abbandando sped to the scene, spotted their nemesis, and opened fire with pistols and a shotgun. Meyer Shapiro took cover and, against all odds, wasn't hurt. Soon two patrol cars were in hot pursuit of the shooters. Sirens blaring, they fired on the suspects' zigzagging car without success. After almost three miles, the hoods hurled their weapons out the window of the automobile and brought it to a screeching halt. Despite the assassination attempt on Meyer Shapiro and the wild car chase, Reles and company were charged only with grand larceny (they'd been riding in a stolen vehicle).

The Shapiro gang retaliated several weeks later. Reles was loafing in front of a poolroom when a car crept by and unleashed a hail of lead; he escaped with only minor cuts from the shattered storefront windows. Reles blew his chance at revenge the following week after spotting Meyer Shapiro walking down a busy Brooklyn street. Without waiting for a clear shot, he opened fire. The terrified crowd scattered. Incredibly, no one was hit. All the slugs lodged harmlessly in a passing car.

September 17, 1931, was the day Meyer Shapiro's luck finally ran out. Reles had begun carefully cultivating a Shapiro gang member known only as "Juey." It seems that Juey knew which way the wind was blowing: As far as he was concerned, the Shapiro gang's days were numbered. Reles welcomed Juey's help, though he worked through intermediaries in order to keep him at arm's length. (After having been burned by Joey Silver, Reles wasn't taking any chances.) Eventually, Juey ingratiated himself with Meyer Shapiro enough to be invited on a walk-and-talk—a stroll where gangland business was discussed. As the two men meandered along, Juey slowed his pace slightly. Absorbed in hearing himself talk, Meyer Shapiro never noticed that his companion had removed a pistol from his waistband. Juey dispatched Meyer—in midsentence—with a single shot behind his left ear.

■■■

When news of Meyer Shapiro's death reached the remaining Shapiro troops—whose number could be counted on one hand—they scattered to the four winds. The war for Brownsville was over.

There was, however, one piece of unfinished business: Willie Shapiro. Terrified and powerless, the last of the brothers had gone into hiding. With no street crew of his own, he was no threat to the new order. But Reles saw things differently. Why take the chance that Willie might seek revenge—or try, someday, to win back a way of life that had been ripped away from him? It took several years, but Reles and his goons finally caught up with Willie in 1934. They beat and tortured him mercilessly, stuffed him in a laundry bag, then buried him alive.

■■■

Abe Reles had achieved his American Dream: He was now the undisputed Boss of Brownsville. He quickly tightened the Combination's grip on its hard-won territory. Extortion from large-scale businesses, such as wholesale bakeries and trucking fleets, was ratcheted up. Gambling revenues soared as slot machines were forcibly installed in poolrooms and candy stores, and bookmaking joints were set up on almost every block. The gang's lifeblood was loan-sharking, or "shylocking." Its loan scheme was known as the six-for-five—a six-dollar fee for every five dollars borrowed for one week. With the average transaction lasting six weeks, Reles and his crew took in an astonishing 120 percent profit on a typical loan. It was expected that a hefty share of the take from all of the Combination's rackets would be tithed to Albert Anastasia. Without question, he'd made it all possible.

To keep pace with the booming business, Reles opened the gang's membership rolls. Among the new inductees were: Louis "Tiny" Benson, a fearsome 420-pound loan shark and debt collector; Sholem Bernstein, a dark-eyed felon who stole the vehicles that were later used as getaway cars; Angelo "Julie" Catalano, a former cabbie who was now an ace wheelman; Irving "Gangy" Cohen, an enforcer whose favorite weapon was an ice pick; Oscar "the Poet" Friedman, an oddball who divided his time between fencing stolen goods and reading classical poetry; Lena and Abraham Frosch, a mother-and-son team who specialized in setting up numbers rackets; Vito "Socko" Gurino, a slob who practiced his marksmanship by shooting the heads off chickens in his backyard; Abe "Pretty" Levine, an extortionist with the good looks of a movie star; Samuel "Red" Levine, a freckle-faced Orthodox Jew enforcer who refused to kill on the Sabbath; Anthony "Dukey" Maffetore, a slow-witted brute who buried his face in comic books between crimes; Seymour Magoon, a ruffian whose perpetual five o'clock shadow earned him the nickname "Blue Jaw"; Walter Sage, a baby-faced gambling wizard; and Meyer "Mickey" Sycoff, a portly but menacing loan shark.

■■■

In retrospect, what makes the Combination's success so galling is that it took place in the midst of the Depression. At a time when honest men and women, haggard and hungry, stood in endless lines at soup kitchens, criminals like Reles were enjoying the good life. There was one thing, though, that Reles and his cohorts desperately wanted but would never attain: prestige. As one newspaper put it at the time: "They never rose from Brownsville flats to penthouses, as have other city gangsters. They never opened any big nightclubs; they never acquired large legitimate business interests."

The Combination's headquarters spoke volumes about its low station in the Mob hierarchy. Reles ran his fiefdom from a back booth in Midnight Rose's, a rundown Brownsville candy store and soda

Midnight Rose's candy store (far right, near elevated train tracks). [NYC Municipal Archives]

fountain under the elevated train tracks at the corner of Saratoga and Livonia avenues—Reles cleverly christened this center of his universe as "the Corner." Here, at Midnight Rose's, he would dole out cash to his shylocks, pass along the names of deadbeats to his enforcers, and plot murders with his lieutenants. The store also served as a bank for the Combination's shylocking operations: In one thirteen-month period, more than four hundred thousand dollars in loan transactions took place here. Outside the store, gangster wannabes loafed around, hoping to be tossed a crumb of an assignment.

Midnight Rose's was owned by Rose Gold, the elderly mother of a local hood. A salty-tongued crone, she kept her joint open around the clock to accommodate the odd hours her customers kept. "Why do you allow hoodlums to hang out in your store?" a reporter once asked. "Why don't the police keep them out?" Rose shot back. If one of the boys got pinched, she would dutifully appear at the lockup, whatever the hour, to bail him out. Rose played the babe-in-the-woods act to the hilt. When she was asked what the notorious "Pittsburgh Phil" Strauss did for a living, her memorable reply was: "Pittsburgh, Chicago, San Francisco . . . what do I know about them? I was never out of Brooklyn in my life."

During his long tenure as director of the FBI, J. Edgar Hoover had to contend with some of the nation's most notorious lawbreakers. When he was asked in 1939 to name "the most dangerous criminal in the United States," Hoover replied, without hesitation, Louis "Lepke" Buchalter. (The name *Lepke*, which struck fear in the hearts of even the most hardened thugs, was bestowed upon him by his mother; it comes from the Yiddish word *Lepkeleh*, or "little Louis.") From the late 1920s through most of the 1930s, Lepke was the czar of labor racketeering in America. In 1932, when he was thirty-five and at the height of his power, he was hauling in ten million dollars a year, a colossal fortune for the times.

How did he bring in this massive sum? With a portfolio that included many obscenely lucrative rackets. The protection scam was an especially profitable one: Lepke's army of thugs—250 strong by many estimates—terrorized manufacturers in Manhattan's vast Garment District into paying mounds of cash to make sure nothing disastrous happened to their merchandise. Reluctant to pay? Count on getting roughed up. Dragging your feet? Expect acid to be splashed on racks of new clothing. Still haven't learned your lesson? This time, the acid gets thrown in your face. Lepke also scored big bucks by exploiting labor unions. Through rigged elections, he would install his stooges in the leadership of key unions (including those representing truckers, taxi drivers, restaurant workers, bakers, and furriers). He would then order them to threaten a company with a potentially crippling strike. When the firm's owners came through with enough money to avoid the work stoppage, the threat was rescinded. Make no mistake about it, though: Lepke was no Robin Hood. He didn't share a penny of his windfalls with the working stiffs he supposedly represented. In fact, he stole from them, too, by skimming from their union dues, and by forcing them to kick back a percentage of their paltry wages to him.

Louis "Lepke" Buchalter. [Collections of the Library of Congress]

Diminutive and sad-eyed, Lepke was considered a towering intellect by his gangland brethren because he'd completed the seventh grade. This achievement made him a brainy giant next to the knuckle-scraping dullards around him. Unlike the comic nicknames given to many underworld figures, Lepke's moniker—Judge Louis—was a sign of the esteem in which he was held.

■■■

The man whom famed racket buster Thomas E. Dewey would one day call "the worst industrial racketeer in America" began life on February 6, 1897, in a Russian-Jewish enclave on the Lower East Side. Lepke's father, Barnett Buchalter, ran a tiny hardware store near the family's tenement flat at 217 Henry Street. His mother, Rose, peddled herring and other foods door-to-door. Despite these humble beginnings, most of the Buchalter children grew up to be model citizens: Lepke's brothers, Emmanuel and Isadore, became, respectively, a dentist and a pharmacist; a half brother became an esteemed rabbi in Denver, while a half sister became a well-regarded schoolteacher.

And then there was Lepke, who turned out as crooked as a dog's hind leg. Surprisingly, the warning signs were not there at first. Lepke was an exemplary pupil in grade school. Though he was deemed to be of only average intelligence, he applied himself assiduously to his schoolwork. Even after his father's sudden death in 1910, and the family's abrupt move to the Williamsburg section of Brooklyn, Lepke always brought home a respectable report card.

By 1912, there was an internal tug-of-war going on for Lepke's soul. On the one hand, he had been arrested for his part in a gang fight (the charges were later dropped); on the other, he took on a grueling job as a delivery boy for three dollars a week—and faithfully turned over his earnings to his mother. Lepke lost the job, however, and with it any desire to go straight. Instead, he spent much of his time back at his old Lower East Side stomping grounds. There, a biographer noted, "he loitered on street corners and frequented poolrooms where he came into contact with underworld characters who began to influence him. Emulating the conduct of his ill-chosen associates, [Lepke] made no effort to find employment, preferring instead to secure his money by joining companions in their exploits as purse snatchers and package thieves." He also began extorting small sums from those eternally hapless targets—pushcart peddlers—and ran errands for neighborhood gangsters.

A glance at Lepke's early rap sheet gave no indication that he would become one of the great criminal masterminds of the twentieth century. In September 1915, he notched his first arrest as an adult—a sort of coming of age among thugs—for burglary and felonious assault. The charges were later dismissed. In January 1916, he was collared for burglary a second time. Once again, the charges were dismissed. In February of that year, his knack for avoiding jail time finally failed him: Lepke was caught with two sample cases packed with jewelry that a careless salesman had left unattended. Convicted of theft of property and sent to a state reformatory, he was paroled after slightly more than a year.

Lepke's life continued downhill at a rapid clip. A January 1918 conviction for grand larceny sent him to the big house: Sing Sing Prison in Ossining, New York. Apparently, the older, more seasoned felons didn't help Lepke hone his criminal skills: He was pinched for burglary just a few months after his January 1919 release—though a curiously sympathetic magistrate tossed out the charges. He managed to get busted for burglary again in January 1920. Incredibly, while out on bail, he was arrested on yet another burglary charge! Having apparently run out of second chances, Lepke was handed a return ticket to Sing Sing— good for eighteen months of confinement.

Paroled in 1922, he decided to embrace the gangster life fully. As his biographer has explained, "Lepke began to appreciate that the loner in the underworld had none of the protection and opportunity afforded those who ran with a gang." He hooked up with an old friend, Jacob "Gurrah" Shapiro, a hulking blockhead from Minsk, who worked as a slugger (or enforcer) for mobster Jacob "Little Augie" Orgen. Little Augie was the tyrannical overlord of Manhattan's Garment District, one of gangland's premier cash cows. He put Gurrah's little buddy on the payroll, even though he fretted over how well the pint-size Lepke would handle the rough stuff his job entailed.

Little Augie should have worried more about himself. "It was during Lepke's apprenticeship to Little Augie that [he] saw the possibilities of entire industries held captive by, and paying tribute to, gangsters in return for protection," wrote Lepke's biographer. He and Shapiro, another commentator noted, began "relentlessly consolidating their positions in the gang, expanding their network of alliances, even as they faithfully carried out their assignments." Lepke, Shapiro, and other renegade members of the gang decided in 1927 that Little Augie had outlived his usefulness. Word trickled down that the boss had begun cozying up to one John Thomas Diamond—better known as "Legs" Diamond—one of the most depraved hoods of the era. For some reason, Little Augie had been handing out contracts for strong-arm work in the Garment District to Diamond's thugs, contracts that rightfully belonged to Little Augie's own troops. The boss was taking food out of the mouths of his own soldiers and giving it to Diamond—an Irishman, no less!

The coup came on the evening of October 15, 1927. Little Augie and Legs Diamond met outside Little Augie's headquarters on the Lower East Side. Before the two hoods could step inside, a black touring car with Lepke at the wheel came to a screeching halt just feet away; out popped Jacob Shapiro, gun blazing. Little Augie crashed to the pavement with a fatal wound to his head. Diamond was hit twice just below the heart but managed to survive. (His luck ran out in 1931, when a rival gangster shot him to pieces in an Albany, New York, rooming house.)

Hearing that they were wanted for questioning in the murder, Lepke and Shapiro sauntered into a police station a few days later. They were grilled intensely by the cops, but they stuck to their carefully rehearsed alibi about having attended a movie the night of the killing. They were released due to lack of evidence. Lepke moved quickly to consolidate his position in the underworld. He wisely combined the remnants of Little Augie's gang with his own growing group of toughs, guaranteeing a smooth transition. All Hail Lepke, the New King of the Labor Rackets!

Approximately fifty thousand people worked in the Garment District, the sprawling city-within-a-city that Lepke inherited from Little Augie. During this era, 60 percent of the clothing worn by Americans was made in New York City (an astonishing figure given today's massive imports from Asia and elsewhere). The garment industry consisted of four major divisions: women's clothing, men's clothing, hats, and furs. Some of the employees were highly skilled, like the cutters who snipped out sections of garments from complex patterns; others were near-robotic workers who repeated the same minute task hundreds or thousands of times each day, such as sewing buttons onto shirtfronts.

Lepke sat at the center of this universe, taking in some ten million dollars a year through the blackmail and extortion of both management and labor. Never one to sit on his hands, he was soon dispatching his dreaded enforcers to gain a chokehold over other industries, such as flour distribution, baking, handbag making, shoemaking, poultry markets, movie theaters, and taxi companies. But Lepke hit the gangland jackpot when he set his sights on the trucking industry. (This was before truckers became members of the Teamsters Union.)

"By seizing control of the trucking business," a student of Lepke's methods has observed, "either through operating his own trucks outright or by placing lieutenants in key positions within the truckers' unions, Lepke had management and labor at his mercy. To avoid a potential paralysis by a truckers' strike, which would force workers out of work and bankrupt the manufacturers, both sides paid handsomely." Lepke may have pulled in as much as one million dollars a year from this racket alone.

In 1931, Lepke married Betty Wasserman, a widow from London. (Precisely how they met is unclear.) The couple lived in the swank Majestic Apartments overlooking Central Park West. Lepke didn't drink, smoke, gamble, or carouse (his greatest indulgence was a yearly trip to the restorative baths in Carlsbad, Czechoslovakia). He was devoted to Betty and Harold, her eight-year-old son from a previous marriage; he even kept a picture of Harold, whom he legally adopted, inside the back cover of his diamond-studded, platinum pocket watch. When he filled out the adoption papers, Lepke listed his annual income as a modest twenty thousand dollars.

■■■

Sometime in 1932, Lepke was searching for some extra muscle to end an intractable wildcat strike (that is, one he hadn't engineered himself). He turned to his friend Albert Anastasia for help; Anastasia in turn called on Abe Reles. "There was some kind of dispute, and we had to go straighten it out," Reles recounted. (None of Reles's troops questioned these outside jobs: "I just obey. It would be more healthier," is how one of them put it.) Reles met the exalted Lepke at his posh office at 200 Fifth Avenue—a world apart from Midnight Rose's candy store—to get his marching orders. After dishing out a few broken kneecaps here and some cracked skulls there, Reles put an end to the dispute. Lepke was so pleased with Reles's work that he later loaned some of his own enforcers—including his trusted lieutenant Albert "Allie" Tannenbaum—to the Combination.

"We did favors for them, and they returned the favors," Reles later explained. The relationship, however, was strictly business: Lepke wouldn't have been caught dead socializing with a cretin like Abe Reles.

As news of Reles's success made its way through the underworld grapevine, Albert Anastasia found himself loaning out his golden boy more and more—even to mobsters outside New York. The 1933 slaying of John Bagdonowitz was Anastasia's "favor" to an out-of-state Mob boss. Bagdonowitz was a low-level New Jersey hood who decided to go straight. Of course, back then no one quit the Mob and lived to tell about it. Bagdonowitz's boss put out a contract on this loose cannon, worried that he might sing to the cops. Try as they might, however, the Jersey boys couldn't find Bagdonowitz. An anxious call went out to Anastasia, who asked Reles to lend a hand. Within days, Reles's contacts informed him that Bagdonowitz was hiding out in a cottage on Long Island. One evening Reles knocked on the cottage door and politely identified himself as a detective to Bagdonowitz's wife. She let him in. It was a blink-of-an-eye mistake that left her a widow.

There has been much pen swinging over the years by writers who claim that Reles and his colleagues were paid a retainer by Mob bosses to act as hit men, or that they were compensated for each individual contract murder. Reles himself emphatically rejected these claims. "You don't get paid for that kind of work," he said. "When you kill, it's duty."

Outside jobs like the Bagdonowitz hit brought Reles his share of glory. But he never lost sight of how important it was to take care of business at home. Even a seemingly trivial offense on the Combination's turf was met with a swift and deadly response. Alex "Red" Alpert learned that lesson the hard way.

On November 25, 1933, Alpert, a nineteen-year-old petty thief, got into a shouting match with Harry Strauss over the value of some stolen jewelry he wanted Strauss to fence. Seething with rage over Alpert's smart mouth, Strauss stormed over to Midnight Rose's, where he commiserated with Reles and Buggsy Goldstein. Reles called over gang member Walter Sage, Alpert's friend, and ordered him to lure his buddy to a prearranged location on Van Siclen Avenue in Brownsville. Less than an hour later, Alpert was shot dead as he strolled to his "meeting" with Sage. Reles, Goldstein, Strauss, and (mistakenly) Dukey Maffetore were charged with Alpert's murder the next day, but the case was dismissed due to lack of evidence.

To Reles and his cohorts, the murder of Red Alpert was just another rubout. In their wildest dreams, they could never have imagined the firestorm that this killing would one day ignite.

■■■

On the morning of February 16, 1934, Reles brought his car into a garage for an oil change. Charles Battle, the attendant, didn't work fast enough to suit Reles, so he smashed a bottle over Battle's head, fracturing his skull (Battle eventually recovered). A jury convicted Reles of third-degree assault (a misdemeanor), and Judge George W. Martin gave him the maximum sentence of three years. Sickened by the brutality of the crime, he also gave Reles a fierce tongue-lashing. Calling him "one of the most vicious characters we have had in Brooklyn in many years," the judge said that Reles was "brave enough to stab in the back, or shoot, a defenseless person," but that he'd "never stand up to a square man-to-man fight. He hasn't got that kind of courage." The judge also predicted that Reles would eventually "be put out of the way by some good detective with a couple of bullets." Only this last remark seemed to get under Reles's skin. "I'll take on any cop with pistols or anything else," he bellowed as bailiffs hustled him away. "A cop counts to fifteen when he puts his finger on the trigger before he shoots."

Reles's time in an upstate New York prison became a mockery of criminal punishment. Loan shark Mickey Sycoff brought him envelopes stuffed with cash for use behind bars; Sycoff also provided Reles's wife with a weekly stipend. Reles's partners made sure his share of the Combination's earnings was socked away until he got out of the joint. And Buggsy Goldstein visited him on a regular basis, bringing the latest gangland news and carrying his orders back to the rank and file.

■■■

In a tough neighborhood like Brownsville, it was a safe bet that some ruffian would try to earn a name for himself by aiming to rub out the top dog. Enter John "Spider" Murtha, one of Reles's most formidable early challengers.

Murtha, a former prizefighter, was as mean as they come. In fact, even the cops at the local precinct were reluctant to tangle with him; many thought he was the odds-on favorite to make Reles's reign as the Boss of Brownsville a brief one. It's not difficult to see why the authorities felt this way. Murtha's rap sheet reads like a pedigree for a professional lowlife. It kicks off with a 1915 arrest for robbery (for which Spider was later "exonerated"), and marches along with arrests for rape and three murders. The only serious time Murtha spent behind bars was a stint he did at Sing Sing for gouging out a rival's eyeball.

Murtha had the distinction of having committed two murders on the same evening but in different locations and under different circumstances. The date was May 3, 1932. He had just sidled up to the bar at a speakeasy that was on his shakedown route. He told the owner, Moe Glickman, that he was raising his fee for "protecting" the establishment. When Glickman balked, Murtha shot him in the face. Still clutching a bar rag, Moe was dead before he hit the floor. Unshaken by this fiendish homicide, Murtha headed to another speakeasy, this time for a social visit. He spotted an attractive young woman, Catherine Pinther, dining with a female friend. Murtha offered to buy Pinther a drink; when she declined, he was so offended that he drew his revolver and shot her dead. As patrons dove for cover and the acrid smell of gunpowder filled the tavern, Murtha calmly walked out and went into hiding. For several months, cops distributed wanted flyers throughout Brooklyn in a halfhearted attempt to find him. But nobody dared to finger Spider Murtha.

Reles knew that Murtha had often voiced the opinion that the members of the Combination weren't so tough—that he, Murtha, could take them out without any effort at all, and that he might just do it someday. Reles, of course, had no intention of spending the rest of his days looking over his shoulder for Spider Murtha's ugly puss. The Glickman and Pinther murders brought the issue of what to do with Murtha to the front burner. Reles approved a hit on Murtha from behind bars. Feelers were put out, and soon the Combination had a fix on the vicious fugitive's Brooklyn hideout.

On the morning of March 3, 1935, Frank Abbandando and Max "the Jerk" Golob, a Combination gunman, were lying in wait outside a rooming house on Atlantic Avenue. When Murtha and his girlfriend, Marie Nestfield, came strolling out, the two hoods ambled up behind them. Nestfield was shoved aside, and the assassins shot Murtha twice in the head and three times in the chest. The bullets slammed Murtha against an el train support column, and he slid to the ground, dead. In a sense, the murders of Moe Glickman and Catherine Pinther had been avenged. Not that Reles gave a damn about those two innocents: Murtha's murder was an act of self-preservation—a preemptive strike in classic gangland fashion.

■■■

In the fall of 1936, Lepke came calling for help once again. This time the problem was Joseph Rosen, the owner of a small trucking company that hauled merchandise from several garment factories. Lepke's recent decree that the factories were to use only Mob-owned trucking companies had forced Rosen's independent firm into bankruptcy. Rosen tried to get back on his feet by opening a small candy store in Brownsville, but it just wasn't enough to pay the bills. Mad as hell, he blabbed to just about everyone within earshot that he would spill the beans about Lepke's criminal deeds to Thomas E. Dewey, the resolute special prosecutor appointed by New York governor Herbert Lehman in 1935 to investigate organized crime. When news of the threat reached Lepke, the normally unflappable mobster blew up. "That son of a bitch Rosen is going around Brownsville, shooting off his mouth about seeing Dewey," he railed. "I'll take care of him."

Several of Lepke's minions tried to talk him out of whacking Rosen, arguing that the former trucker was insignificant in the scheme of things. But the boss was adamant: Rosen had to go. He gave the contract to Emanuel "Mendy" Weiss, his most trusted deputy, on September 11, 1936.

Weiss quickly assembled a hit team. He chose Harry Strauss to be the shooter, Louis Capone to plot out the escape route, and Sholem Bernstein to be the wheelman. After Bernstein stole a sedan to be used as the getaway car, Capone joined him for a leisurely drive along Sutter Avenue in Brownsville.

"That is where somebody is going to get killed," Capone said in a matter-of-fact way, pointing to Rosen's store. No names were mentioned. He then had Bernstein drive the escape route until it became second nature.

"He showed me the route again and again," Bernstein later recalled. "Seven or eight times we went over it." Capone knew that there could be no room for error on a contract handed down by Lepke himself.

At around 7:00 a.m. on Sunday, September 13, 1936, Rosen was unlocking his candy store when Weiss and Strauss slipped in and eviscerated him with ten bullets fired at point-blank range. Before the few people on the street realized what had happened, the killers hopped into the waiting sedan and were whisked away. Everything went off like clockwork. Lepke was delighted when he got the news. Another perfect crime. Or so it seemed.

■■■

Reles was set free from Sing Sing in March 1937, after serving his sentence for the vicious assault on gas station attendant Charles Battle in 1934. He was soon back in the swing of things in Brownsville.

George "Whitey" Rudnick, a small-time loan shark, had known Reles since they were boyhood pals serving time together at the Elmira reformatory. In May 1937, Harry Strauss caught a glimpse of Rudnick getting out of a police car. Could Whitey be a snitch? Reles wasn't about to waste time finding out, even though his friend's life was at stake. For three nights, Reles and Frank Abbandando staked out Rudnick's regular haunts, to no avail. Finally, in the early morning hours of May 25, they saw Rudnick near Midnight Rose's. Reles and Abbandando lured him into a car and drove to the Sunrise Garage in Ocean Hill, where Harry Strauss, Happy Maione, and Angelo Catalano were waiting. Reles stayed outside as a lookout for pesky cops and nosy passersby. When Rudnick entered the garage, Strauss stabbed him repeatedly with an ice pick. As the killers stuffed the victim into the backseat of a stolen car, he seemed to gasp slightly.

"The bum ain't dead yet," Strauss snarled, jamming his ice pick into Rudnick's throat. For good measure, Maione then split open the victim's head with a cleaver.

"That oughta fix the bum up," Maione said with satisfaction. Catalano then drove the stolen car a few miles away and abandoned it— with the bloody cargo that was once George Rudnick still crammed into the backseat.

A few months later, the Combination had to mete out justice to one of its own. Walter Sage was in charge of the gang's burgeoning gambling operations in the Catskills. In the summer of 1937, Reles concluded that Sage was dipping into the take; he decided to relieve Walter of his managerial duties for good. Sage was driven to a remote spot in the Catskills where Harry Strauss stabbed him thirty-two times with an ice pick. A slot machine was lashed to Sage's corpse, and the hefty bundle tossed into a lake. Strauss believed that the one-armed bandit would keep the body permanently submerged, but ten days later Sage's decomposing cadaver floated to the surface. When Strauss read in the newspapers that Sage had bobbed to the surface despite the plethora of deep puncture wounds, he was dumbfounded: "With this bum, you gotta be a doctor, or he floats!"

In 1937, Jacob "Yasha" Katzenberg was denounced as an "international menace" by the League of Nations. He was accused of directing a vast heroin-smuggling network that had been operating since 1930. Katzenberg's agents obtained the heroin in China and shipped it to Marseilles, where they packed the junk into steamer trunks and transported it to Cherbourg. There it was placed aboard luxury liners like the *Queen Mary* and the *Aquitania* for the Atlantic crossing to New York City. The enterprise brought in upward of ten million dollars a year once the heroin was cut at a Mob lab in the Bronx and sold to addicts on the street. In 1935, the venture attracted the interest of Lepke Buchalter, an entrepreneurial sort always on the lookout for new ways to lie, cheat, and steal for profit.

Lepke decided to muscle in on Katzenberg's operation. In exchange for a cut of the profits, he would provide the bribe money that was passed to US customs officials in New York. When Katzenberg hesitated, Lepke arranged for the operative who was handling the payoffs to vanish. Katzenberg got the message. Soon Lepke was pocketing *one-third* of the drug ring's profits in exchange for a paltry sum for bribes. That's what happened when Lepke became one's business partner.

The heroin smuggling was a sweet operation—until the League of Nations denounced Yasha Katzenberg. Such high-profile attention was just the kind of spotlight mobsters detested and feared: It could alert prosecutors that a potentially career-making case was ripe for the picking. Sure enough, a federal probe was soon under way. The investigation gained intensity when the girlfriend of one of the smugglers, bitter over her beau's two-timing ways, ratted out the details of Katzenberg's operation to the Federal Bureau of Narcotics (forerunner of today's Drug Enforcement Administration).

Through his political connections—and he had many—Lepke learned that he was virtually certain to be indicted as part of the smuggling ring. A conviction could mean up to fourteen years in prison. Worse,

Katzenberg, faced with the possibility of doing that kind of hard time, folded like a cheap tent. He agreed to plead guilty and testify against Lepke.

Special Prosecutor Thomas E. Dewey didn't want the feds to have all the glory. He ratcheted up his own investigation of the labor rackets boss. Dewey, a historian has written, "conducted midnight raids on union and company offices and seized their books. He tapped telephones and subpoenaed hundreds of witnesses. Anyone connected to Lepke was brought in, questioned, threatened with indictments and put under enormous pressure to talk."

The full-bore assault was also directed at Lepke himself. His office was kept under constant surveillance, his phones were tapped, and undercover cops followed his every move. The heat became so intense that he was forced to conduct his business in public places like hotel lobbies, subway and el platforms, and even restaurant restrooms. Hardly a day passed when the publicity-hungry Dewey failed to make public pronouncements about taking down Lepke's evil empire and "bringing all the culprits to heel."

Soon Dewey had collected enough evidence to persuade a grand jury to indict Lepke for extortion in both the baking and trucking industries. The possible penalty: thirty years to life. Faced with the nightmarish prospect of spending the rest of his days locked in a prison cell, Lepke did what any stand-up, tough-as-nails Mob boss would do in the same situation: He ran like hell.

Overnight he became the target of a massive international manhunt. The NYPD assigned twenty-five of its most experienced detectives to find him, and the FBI created a special task force to do the same. Close to one million wanted posters offering twenty-five thousand dollars for Lepke—dead or alive—were circulated. (The cash bounty would be doubled within a few months.) With dreams of reward money dancing in their heads, folks claimed to have seen the fugitive in diners and hotels and department stores in nearly every state in the Union. Others swore they'd caught sight of him in England, Poland, and various countries in Latin America and the Caribbean.

But nobody ever collected the bounty on Lepke's head. The truth is that he never left Brooklyn the entire two years—from July 1937 to August 1939—when he was on the lam. And who did the Mob's top echelon entrust with the daunting task of helping Lepke disappear? Who did they believe had the tremendous cunning and nerves of steel that were needed? Perhaps most important of all, who would keep his mouth shut about what was going on? It was Abe Reles on all scores.

Demonstrating his deep disdain for the police, Reles chose a series of hidden-in-plain-sight locations for the most wanted man in the world. These included an empty upstairs office at the Oriental Danceland, a Coney Island dive owned by Zaccarino "Big Zack" Cavitola (a cousin of Louis Capone, Albert Anastasia's trusted lieutenant). After several months, Lepke was moved in the dead of night to an apartment at Foster Avenue, where Dorothy Walker, the elderly widow of gangster Simon "Fatty" Walker, was only too happy to help in exchange for rent money. The final lair was a basement apartment in a house on 13th Street owned by Maria Nostrio, a friend of Albert Anastasia from the Old Country.

What spurred Reles to move his precious cargo from one hideout to another when he did? We may never know. What we do know is that Reles met with Lepke at least twice a week at these hideouts to brief him on the latest Mob business. A considerate visitor, he always brought a supply of Coronas and a box of chocolates. (True to his tight-fisted nature, however, Reles charged the cost of his largesse to Mendy Weiss's account at Midnight Rose's candy store.) To keep Lepke from going stir-crazy, Reles occasionally took him on clandestine nighttime drives around Brooklyn.

As the months wore on, it became clear that living on the lam was not Lepke's strong suit. He was accustomed to the finer things in life, and now there were none to be had. Worse, his guts were twisted in knots from the fear that some of his old cronies would fold under Thomas Dewey's pressure and agree to testify against him. He decided to ease his mind—and improve his odds—by whacking anyone he thought might conceivably sell him out. "No witnesses, no indictments," became his credo. In a throwback to the good old days, he called on Reles to get things rolling. The resulting murder spree—in which at least twelve people were killed between 1937 and 1939—was a collaborative effort carried out by members of Reles's crew and some of Lepke's goons.

One of the men slated for assassination was Philip Orlovsky, an associate of Lepke's in the garment industry. When rumors reached Lepke that Orlovsky might be squealing to Dewey's investigators, he handed down a death sentence. The assignment was given to Buggsy Goldstein, one of the cofounders of the Combination. On July 25, 1939, Goldstein pumped six bullets into Orlovsky as he left his Bronx apartment for work. Well, it *looked* like Orlovsky. When the newspapers came out, however, Goldstein learned that he had murdered forty-two-year-old Irving Penn, an executive in the music publishing industry. Penn had no connection to Lepke or the underworld. However, he did have the double misfortune of living in the same building as Orlovsky and resembling the intended victim. Never had gangster Ben Siegel's dictum "We only kill each other" rung so hollow.

The Penn murder spurred J. Edgar Hoover to proclaim Lepke Public Enemy No. 1. It also caused a rare display of emotion on the part of the normally taciturn Dewey. "It is apparent that the Lepke Mob is waging a war of extermination against its former and some of its present members," he angrily told the press. Naturally, Reles had a different take on things: "Lepke was satisfied real good," he later boasted of his role in directing the murder spree.

One of the rubouts that year would come back to haunt Albert Anastasia in a major way. It all began when Lepke convinced himself that Morris Diamond, business manager of a Teamster local, was planning to betray him. Clearly, Diamond's time had come. For reasons that remain unclear to this day, Anastasia became personally involved in planning the hit. This didn't fit the mold for a couple of reasons: First, the beef with Diamond didn't involve Anastasia, and second, Mob bosses rarely became directly involved in the details of a contract murder. Yet Anastasia chose the site for the assassination, tapped waterfront thug Gioacchino "Dandy Jack" Parisi to be the triggerman, and picked the ubiquitous Angelo Catalano to drive the getaway car.

Anastasia learned that Diamond left for work each morning at the same time, and that he passed a busy intersection on his way to the subway station. The day before the hit, Anastasia, Parisi, and Catalano piled into Anastasia's car for a field trip to the spot where Diamond's life would end. Anastasia pulled the car over near the intersection. After briefly surveying the scene, he turned to Catalano.

"Tomorrow morning, park right here," he told the former cabbie. "Jackie [Parisi] will be over there, on the northwest corner, like he's waiting for a bus. When he sees Diamond, he'll start walking across. You start up the car. When he hits Diamond, be right there on the crossing so he can jump in." It was a brazen plan, all the more so because it would be carried out in broad daylight.

On the early morning of May 25, 1939, Catalano drove to the pre-arranged spot. The killers were in a cheery mood. "A block from the corner," Catalano remembered, "I see Albert parked in his car. I holler 'hello' and he waves back to me." Parisi was in position, pretending to be engrossed in a newspaper. When he spotted Diamond, he slipped his gun into the paper and stepped off the curb. Catalano slowly rolled toward the intersection. Parisi reached the opposite sidewalk just as Diamond arrived; he raised his concealed pistol and emptied it into the victim's back. As Catalano pulled away with Parisi on board, Diamond died crawling along the sidewalk.

While Lepke was busy playing a god, deciding which of his supposed enemies would die, his *friends* were scheming to sell him out. FBI director Hoover, livid at coming up empty in the manhunt, let Mob bosses across the nation know that unless Lepke turned himself in immediately, the FBI would haul *them* in on any and every charge imaginable. It was a spectacle the bosses desperately wanted to avoid. Word was sent to Lepke that the jig was up. When Allie Tannenbaum visited the boss in July 1939, he was stunned to learn that Lepke had "received an ultimatum in a nice way to either walk in [surrender] or else." Tannenbaum couldn't believe that the boss's peers would force one of their own to give up "under pain of death." Gloomily, Lepke said that they were doing just that. Despite the grim news, the rackets boss was magnanimous, telling Tannenbaum that turning himself in might be "the best thing" because it would "save you kids from a lot of trouble."

The bosses did offer a small spoonful of honey to go with the huge dose of castor oil: They promised that if Lepke surrendered to Hoover on the federal narcotics charge, the FBI chief would see to it that he received a reduced sentence of perhaps ten years. More importantly, Hoover would refuse to turn Lepke over to Dewey for trial on the racketeering charges that could send him away for life. Reles and Anastasia smelled a trap and urged Lepke to turn the deal down. (As Anastasia put it: "While they ain't got you, they can't hurt you.") But after nearly two years on the run, Lepke had little or no fight left in him.

Enter Walter Winchell. One of the most powerful celebrity gossip scribes of his day—some two thousand newspapers carried his column—Winchell hosted a hugely popular weekly radio show heard by millions of Americans. And he was a friend of J. Edgar Hoover. Perhaps that's why on the evening of August 5, 1939, Winchell received a phone call as he held court at the swank Stork Club in Manhattan. The caller was clearly someone accustomed to giving orders.

"Don't ask who I am," he growled. "I have something to tell you. Lepke wants to come in." The caller then instructed Winchell to obtain J. Edgar Hoover's personal guarantee that Lepke wouldn't be harmed if he tried to surrender. (Lepke's die-hard supporters, including Reles, were concerned that some trigger-happy FBI agent might take a shot at him for the glory of gunning down Public Enemy No. 1.)

Hoover in turn gave Winchell the desired guarantee. But he wasn't about to let his buddy the gossipmonger steal the spotlight. Hoover and a team of FBI agents immediately headed to New York. They registered at the Waldorf-Astoria Hotel, armed to the teeth and ready to swoop down on Lepke as soon as he showed his face.

On August 6, Winchell took to the airwaves to announce that "Lepke, the fugitive, is on the verge of surrender, perhaps this week. I am authorized by the feds [to say] that Lepke is assured of safe delivery." The Mob was listening. For the next few days, Winchell and his underworld contact spoke by phone regularly, seeking to finalize every detail of the plan for Lepke's surrender.

Over the next few weeks, Winchell was sent on several wild goose chases by his caller. (He believed members of the Mob were trailing him to these locations to see if he was traveling alone.) The gossip columnist was directed to await a call at a certain pay phone; that call directed him to another pay phone, and so on. On one occasion, Winchell, finding himself alone in a vacant lot in New Jersey at 3:00 a.m., got spooked and left the scene. When Hoover learned about the incident, he decided he'd had enough of this cat-and-mouse game. "You can tell your friends," the FBI director barked at Winchell, "that if Lepke isn't in within forty-eight hours, I will order my agents to shoot him on sight." When Winchell repeated Hoover's threat to his underworld caller, it was greeted with derisive laughter. "You people haven't been able to find him in two years," he chortled. "How you gonna find him in forty-eight hours?"

The end of Lepke's two-year vanishing act was like something out of a spy novel. On the night of August 24, 1939, the phone at the Stork Club rang; the caller asked for the ever-present Winchell. The columnist was given an address in Yonkers and told to head there immediately. A car full of shady characters was waiting for him at the site. One of the occupants, whose face was partially covered by a bandanna like an outlaw from the Old West, passed along an address of a Manhattan drugstore. Winchell was to head back into the city and await further instructions there.

As Winchell waited at the pharmacy, a stranger on the sidewalk motioned for him to come outside. The mystery man told Winchell to call J. Edgar Hoover (still ensconced at the Waldorf-Astoria) and advise the FBI chief to move his car into position at Fifth Avenue and 23rd Street by 10:00 p.m. He then had Winchell drop him off at Madison Avenue and 24th Street, telling the columnist to remain at that location. The stranger then disappeared into the night.

An hour earlier in Brooklyn, Albert Anastasia had picked up Lepke at his hideout. At 10:15 p.m., they rolled up alongside Winchell's vehicle and Lepke climbed inside. Several minutes later, Winchell and Lepke pulled in behind Hoover's sedan on Fifth Avenue. Winchell stuck his head into the car. "Mr. Hoover, this is Lepke," he announced. Hoover was silent. "Nice to meet you," Public Enemy No. 1 said flatly. "Now let's go."

Lepke had barely settled into the backseat when he realized that he'd been snookered by his fellow organized crime bosses: Hoover claimed he knew nothing about a deal that would give the crime boss a reduced sentence if convicted on the heroin smuggling rap. Nor did he know of any agreement to keep him from the clutches of Thomas Dewey and his racketeering indictments. Reles and Anastasia had been right: Lepke had been duped into surrendering. And there wasn't a damn thing he could do about it now.

In December 1939, Lepke was convicted on the heroin smuggling charge—his former "partner" Yasha Katzenberg was the star witness against him—and given the maximum sentence of fourteen years at Leavenworth Penitentiary. In March 1940, Dewey convicted him on fifteen counts of extortion in the baking and trucking industries; he was slapped with an additional thirty years to life, to be served *after* he'd completed his earlier sentence. It was a shattering one-two punch for the once untouchable Lepke. Indeed, it's hard to imagine that things could still have gotten any worse for him. But they did. Much worse.

■■■

Reles and the Combination lost a friend and benefactor when Lepke was locked up. But Albert Anastasia was still the Mob's power broker in Brooklyn, and Reles was eager to keep him happy. (As he put it: "Albert puts the pressure on for us. Even if we're wrong, he can make it right.") The sadistic murder of a poor slob named Irving "Puggy" Feinstein was just one way Reles showed his abiding respect for Anastasia.

In August 1939, Puggy (whose flat nose was a memento of his brief career as a boxer) set up a loan-sharking venture in Brooklyn. It was penny-ante stuff, and he foolishly believed Anastasia wouldn't notice. He was wrong. Puggy was a problem, and Anastasia told Reles to solve it. Reles's crew searched high and low for Puggy, but they couldn't find him. Then, on the evening of September 4, 1939, Reles, Harry Strauss, Buggsy Goldstein, and Dukey Maffetore were loafing around Midnight Rose's. Who should come strolling along but Puggy! The former boxer was looking for one of the Combination's loan sharks so that he could repay a debt. Reles couldn't believe his good fortune. He ordered

Goldstein and Maffetore to drive Puggy around town, pretending to search for the loan shark. After an hour, they were to bring him to Reles's home. Goldstein and Maffetore drove off with Puggy while Reles headed home with Strauss.

When they arrived, Reles awakened his elderly mother-in-law and asked where he could find some rope and an ice pick. After giving her son-in-law the two items, she wandered into the living room to see what was going on. Strauss, ever the gentleman, told her to get lost. He then pulled up a chair next to the front door, keeping himself hidden from sight; Reles sat in full view to attract Puggy's attention. When Goldstein and Maffetore arrived with Puggy a short time later, Strauss shot out of his chair and threw Puggy to the floor, where Reles swiftly bound him up in a "rope-job"—which causes the victim to strangle himself as he fights for his life—then turned on a radio to drown out his choked pleas for mercy. (Reles thoughtfully slid a newspaper under the victim's chin to prevent the bloody froth oozing from Puggy's mouth from staining the rug.) After Puggy's death throes ceased, Strauss noticed that his hand had been bitten during the struggle. He was petrified. "Maybe I'll get lockjaw from being bit!" he wailed. Reles came to the rescue with a bottle of mercurochrome.

The horror didn't end there. Strauss wanted Puggy's body burned to hinder the identification process. Goldstein drove Puggy's corpse to a vacant lot, doused it with gasoline, and set it ablaze. The killers then met at a favorite seafood restaurant, where they good-naturedly criticized each other's shortcomings in whacking Puggy. The banter stopped when dinner arrived: The boys had worked up quite an appetite, and they tore into their lobsters with a vengeance.

"Murder is safe in Brooklyn," Thomas E. Dewey declared in 1938. "Two out of every three murders remain unsolved. Two out of every three murderers are never indicted; [they] walk the streets as free men."

Just how rotten things were in Brooklyn became clear even before Dewey's comments. On the night of March 3, 1935, police responded to calls of a disturbance at a garage in the Williamsburg neighborhood. The responding cops came upon the wreckage of a human being: beaten with a sawed-off pool cue, garrotted with a rope, and lying in an expanding pool of blood. Three suspects were arrested at the scene—Meyer Luckman, his nephew Harry, and another man. Harry Luckman had fresh bloodstains on his clothes and hands. The subsequent investigation revealed that the victim, Samuel Druckman, had worked for the Mob-connected Luckmans' trucking firm and was suspected of embezzling company funds.

What seemed like an open-and-shut case took an almost incomprehensible turn. Brooklyn district attorney William F. X. Geoghan, a Democrat, presented the murder case to a grand jury—which promptly voted not to indict the accused. The Luckmans were sent on their way, but not before their bloodstained clothing was returned to them.

The outcome of the Druckman affair, as one historian of New York City politics has written, "was too flagrant to pass. Rumors of payoffs and police collaboration were rife. After studying records of the Druckman case, Police Commissioner Lewis J. Valentine became convinced that police officers had destroyed evidence and delivered bribes to the grand jury." In a letter to Brooklyn DA Geoghan, Valentine wrote that his own investigation had revealed the name of the crooked cop who passed bribe money from the Mob to police in the Druckman case. He pressured the DA to reinvestigate the matter in light of his findings—"What kind of crime do you have to commit in Brooklyn to obtain an indictment?" the frustrated Valentine asked rhetorically. But DA Geoghan adamantly refused to resubmit the case to a grand jury.

The scandal reached a critical juncture in December 1935. New York governor Herbert Lehman, infuriated by Geoghan's intractability, appointed a special prosecutor to supersede the Brooklyn DA. The appointee, attorney Hiram C. Todd, didn't fool around: Within six weeks, the Luckmans' good fortune had run out. They were tried and convicted for the Druckman murder. Todd didn't stop there. He convinced a newly empaneled grand jury to indict the son of one of Geoghan's assistant DAs on charges of improperly influencing the grand jury that had first heard the Druckman case. By the time Todd completed his investigation of that bloody night in the Brooklyn garage, eight more individuals were charged with bribery, including the assistant DA whose son had already been charged, a detective, and several mobsters. The grand jury also demanded that Geoghan be removed from office, citing incompetence, negligence, and associating with known hoodlums. Governor Lehman, however, wasn't convinced that removal was necessary, and he declined to take any action against the embattled district attorney.

By the spring of 1938, DA Geoghan thought the worst was over. He joked to reporters that his office didn't have much work because criminals in Brooklyn didn't seem to be committing serious crimes anymore. His career as a comedian was short-lived. The Citizens Committee on the Control of Crime in New York City, founded in 1936 and headed by philanthropist Harry F. Guggenheim, revealed that it had tracked some fourteen thousand cases through the courts in Brooklyn and found "widespread irregularities." The committee's shocking report caused Governor Lehman to supersede Geoghan once again. John Harlan Amen, a special assistant to the attorney general of the United States, Homer S. Cummings, was named special prosecutor. Within months, the dogged Amen "bared a crooked braid, knotting together police, magistrates, appellate court judges, gamblers, loan sharks, and such powerful racketeers as Abe Reles and Lepke Buchalter. He handed up indictments against a new batch of tainted assistant district attorneys and police." The Brooklyn Democratic political machine, which appeared to have slept through the Geoghan scandals, finally awoke from its slumber. The party's power brokers vehemently urged the DA to resign, but the petulant Geoghan refused at first to even entertain the idea. Eventually, he yielded to the unrelenting pressure, and agreed to retire at the end of his term in the fall of 1939. This suited the Democrats just fine: 1939 was an election year, and they would have an opportunity to redeem themselves by nominating a candidate who was, at least to their way of seeing things, squeaky clean.

■■■

Nothing in William O'Dwyer's early life hinted at a future in crime fighting, especially not one knee-deep in the cesspool of the Brooklyn underworld. Born in Ireland in 1890, O'Dwyer was the first of eleven children. Acting on his mother's wishes, he studied for the priesthood during his late teens at the venerable Jesuit University of Salamanca, Spain. But he left without graduating and, loath to face his parents, set sail for America. In 1910, the twenty-year-old O'Dwyer landed in New York City. He worked at a variety of jobs (bartender, deckhand on a freighter, plasterer) before joining the New York City Police Department in 1917. During his off-hours, O'Dwyer earned a law degree. In 1926, he turned in his badge and entered private practice. In the 1930s, he returned to public service, first as a city magistrate, then as a county court judge. Along the way, O'Dwyer earned a reputation for being tough but fair-minded.

O'Dwyer, a Democrat, popped up on the radar of the party's power brokers, who were eager to put the Geoghan nightmare to rest. Impressed by O'Dwyer's diverse experience in law enforcement, party elders urged him to step down from his judicial post and run for district attorney of Brooklyn. Even though the move would mean a drastic pay cut and a substantially shorter term of office, O'Dwyer agreed.

A charismatic public speaker, O'Dwyer ran a robust campaign that focused heavily on combating organized crime. He railed against the "vicious criminals and cheap punks" who were having a field day in the borough. "The number of homicides not solved by the police was astonishing," he noted. "The hoodlums would be arrested with great fanfare,

William O'Dwyer. [Collections of the Library of Congress]

brought before magistrates' Court, and charged with disorderly conduct—nothing more. If you set bail at one thousand dollars, they put their hands in their pockets, peeled off one thousand dollars, and walked out. This had been going on for years."

O'Dwyer blamed the nightmarish state of affairs on crooked judges who were tossing out serious charges—even murder—against hard-core criminals due to "lack of evidence." Enough was enough. "If everybody stays on his toes," he thundered, "the professional racketeer, gunman and hoodlum, who stands out on the street corner like a lighthouse, could not remain in Brooklyn for one minute." By portraying himself as a modern-day Wyatt Earp who would run the bad guys out of town on a rail, O'Dwyer won the election handily against his Republican opponent.

Once in office, O'Dwyer assembled a team of assistant DAs whose goal was to cripple the Mob. He hired a dynamic thirty-eight-year-old trial lawyer named Burton Turkus to head up the homicide division. When Turkus entered his new office for the first time, he was taken aback by a large map of Brooklyn tacked to the wall by his predecessor. There was a mark on the map for each unsolved murder committed in the borough in the previous ten years. The Combination's territory—Brownsville and Ocean Hill—was a veritable thicket of marks. Turkus was aghast. "It was a blighted area—a pesthole," he recalled. "In one strip less than two miles long and three-quarters of a mile wide, two dozen or more men had been shot, stabbed, strangled, hacked to bits or cremated, and left in the gutter, on vacant lots or in stolen automobiles."

After poring over the dusty files on these unsolved murders, Turkus learned that Reles, Harry Strauss, Buggsy Goldstein, Happy Maione, and Frank Abbandando were the prime suspects in most of the killings. But Geoghan, the previous DA, had shown little interest in going after any of them. The situation was complicated by the fact that witnesses tended to develop amnesia once they envisioned an enraged Reles hell-bent on silencing them. Turkus began to fear that O'Dwyer may have promised more than he could deliver when it came to taking on the Mob.

O'Dwyer didn't help his cause when, after realizing there would be no quick fixes, he resorted to the hackneyed tactic of hassling the hoods. "Toughs were yanked unceremoniously off the street corners at every opportunity and charged with any 'rap' on which we could bring them in," Turkus remembered. To Reles, the harassment was like a huge neon sign advertising O'Dwyer's impotence. Far from being alarmed, Reles laughed it all off. "You've got one hell of a nerve," he wisecracked to a cop who hauled him in for vagrancy in January 1940. "First thing you know I'll have to walk around with a bondsman." Shaking his head in mock disbelief, Reles paid his bail from a wad of cash and went free.

To Happy Maione, the harassment was no laughing matter. "If O'Dwyer don't stop pushing us around," he told one of his minions, "we'll start dropping packages on every lot in Brooklyn. That's going to keep him really busy." The DA knew that *package* was underworld lingo for a corpse, and he didn't take the threat lightly.

Just a few short weeks later, everything changed. Among the many letters O'Dwyer's office received every day from crime victims, tipsters, and kooks was a cryptic note from Harry Rudolph, a gravely ill jailbird with a story he had to get off his chest before he died. "I would like to talk to the district attorney," he wrote. "I know something about a murder."

Turkus traveled to Rikers Island to meet the slightly loopy Rudolph, who tearfully recounted an all-but-forgotten crime: the 1933 murder of Alex "Red" Alpert, the petty thief who'd dared to shoot his mouth off to Harry Strauss over some stolen jewels.

"Those rats killed my friend," Rudolph wept. "I'll tell you who did it, too. Those Brownsville guys—Reles and Buggsy Goldstein and

Dukey Maffetore." (Rudolph mistakenly named Dukey instead of Harry Strauss.)

Turkus reviewed the case file and discovered that the trio Rudolph named had been arrested for the Alpert murder, but were later released on the tired "lack of evidence" excuse. Turkus saw this case as a chance to make good on O'Dwyer's promise to get tough on organized crime. Wasting no time, he went before a grand jury just hours after his meeting with Rudolph and obtained first-degree murder indictments against Reles, Goldstein, and Maffetore.

O'Dwyer decided that an in-your-face approach to the Alpert case might give his crusade a much-needed shot in the arm. So he showed up on February 2, 1940, to watch the defendants as they were booked at a local police station, fingerprinted at police headquarters, and arraigned at the courthouse.

"This is a clean-cut charge," O'Dwyer boasted to reporters. "I have an airtight case against these punks and I want them to know it." He made clear the larger implications of the three arrests. "We are planning to clean out the whole racketeering mess," he declared. "This one case will be the wedge. We want to get to the heart of the situation, to clean it all out."

O'Dwyer roundly condemned the Brownsville neighborhood as an incubator of criminal activity. Sensing that he'd gotten carried away by his own rhetoric, he pulled back: "This is not a reflection on the people as a whole of that or any other area. We are going to help the people there who have been crying for assistance a long time."

If Reles and Goldstein were spooked by O'Dwyer's presence, they didn't show it. *The bum's got nothing,* their matching smirks seemed to say. To them, it was just another "tickle"—Mobspeak for an arrest that is designed to get under a crook's skin. At the arraignment, a high-powered attorney appeared on behalf of Reles and Goldstein, and the two thugs pled not guilty.

But nobody showed up to represent Dukey Maffetore. He was forced to request a court-appointed public defender. He, too, pled not guilty, but the fact that the higher-ups in the Mob hadn't sent anyone to help him was a rude awakening. In his childlike way, Dukey always felt that he had a special bond with Reles and Goldstein, like the inseparable Three Musketeers he'd read about in his beloved comic books. Now he knew that it had all been a sham.

O'Dwyer asked the judge to deny bail to all three suspects and to send them to separate jails to prevent them from scheming with one another; both requests were granted. Not by chance, Reles got the worst accommodations. He was remanded to the Tombs jail in Manhattan. Built in 1902, the Tombs was a dungeon-like hole where, as Burton Turkus put it, "even the air smelled of locked doors, barred windows, and hopeless men."

Convinced that Reles and Goldstein would never crack, detectives leaned on the jittery Maffetore. *Why didn't the big shots get you a lawyer, Dukey? Smarten up, for chrissakes! They're gonna make* you *take the fall for the Alpert hit and you wasn't even in on it! Thing is, kid, you could get the chair for this one.* After planting these terrifying images in Dukey's head, detectives tossed him back into "cold storage," aka solitary confinement, to mull over the big-time jam he was in. Maffetore was so frightened of Reles that even though he was facing the death penalty for a crime he didn't commit, he endured this war of nerves for several weeks rather than talk. When Dukey finally caved, he confessed to stealing the car that was used to dispose of Whitey Rudnick's mutilated corpse, and to driving Puggy Feinstein to his death at Reles's home. As the questioning continued, however, it became clear to the DA's men that Maffetore was small potatoes. He didn't have the kind of inside information against the leaders of the Combination that O'Dwyer was after.

Maffetore panicked when the DA's men seemed to lose interest in him. Fearing that they might toss him back on the street, he tried to get back in their good graces by suggesting that Abe "Pretty" Levine, one of his Combination cronies, might be willing to squeal. Why? Because Levine was still fuming over a beef he'd had with Reles. Levine had gone to Reles to borrow money for his pregnant wife's medical bills. Even though the amount was a pittance, Reles demanded the same astronomical interest on the loan that he charged any poor schmuck on the street. Levine was furious—he'd risked the electric chair more than once doing Reles's dirty work—but he knew to keep his mouth shut and pay what Reles demanded.

So Pretty Levine was dragged in and given the third degree. The detectives knew that he was devoted to his wife and baby daughter, so they toyed with his concern for their welfare. *What happens if you gotta do time? How are you gonna support your family? You can bet your ass that if Reles goes away, his family will be taken care of. But yours, they better be able to survive on the street 'cause that's where they're gonna end up.* Still, Levine wouldn't fold. So the cops played hardball: They tossed his wife in jail as a material witness. Levine was incensed, but his fear of Reles was so great that he let his beloved stay locked up for two weeks before he finally gave in. Levine offered some new morsels, including useful information about the murder of Walter Sage in the Catskills. To O'Dwyer's frustration, however, it became clear that Levine, like Maffetore, was just another petty crook who followed orders but never gave them. The DA was back to square one. Turkus, for his part, felt that the plan to smash the Mob was about to collapse "unless we got a top mobster who had all the answers—and would give them out loud."

As if on cue, a distraught young pregnant woman walked into the DA's office in the late afternoon of March 22, 1940—Good Friday. "I want to save my husband from the electric chair," she sobbed. "My baby is coming in June." The previous day, she'd visited her spouse in the Tombs jail. "Go and see O'Dwyer and tell him I want to talk to him," he'd told her gravely. The woman was Rose Reles—Abe's wife!

O'Dwyer and Turkus reacted swiftly. Fearing that it was only a matter of time before the Mob learned of Reles's intentions, they flew through the paperwork required to bring him into protective custody. First, they drew up a Consent Order stating that Reles had voluntarily requested to meet with them. The order was rushed to Reles in his cell; he signed it "as nonchalantly as a celebrity obliging an autograph fan," Turkus related. Next, a court order transferring Reles to the DA's custody was quickly secured. When the time came to make the transfer, it was done under cover of darkness to foil a possible assassination attempt. By 9:00 p.m., a heavily armed NYPD motorcade, led by Captains Frank Bals and John J.

McGowan—two of O'Dwyer's closest friends from his cop days—was speeding Abe Reles to the Brooklyn DA's office.

When Reles arrived, he made himself at home. He slumped in a chair, called for a cigarette, then puffed away contentedly. He seemed tickled that O'Dwyer, Turkus, and several detectives were waiting intently for him to open up. He demanded that his "bracelets" be removed, but a detective told him he would stay cuffed. Then he began looking around the office as if he were sizing up the decor. O'Dwyer got fed up. He tried to puncture Reles's cockiness by confronting him with Harry Rudolph's statement tying him to the Alpert murder.

"That Rudolph—I could make a monkey out of him myself," Reles sniggered. Next, Turkus took a shot at cutting Reles down to size. He tried to hang the gruesome murder of Puggy Feinstein squarely around Reles's neck.

"You can't touch me on that one," Reles replied, flashing a smarmy smile. "You ain't got no corroboration." Reles may have been a cheeky bastard, but he was right: In order to obtain a murder conviction in New York, the law required the corroborating testimony of a non-accomplice to the crime. And that was something the DA simply didn't have.

Suddenly, Reles made his move. Stubbing out his cigarette, he turned to O'Dwyer and said: "I can make you the biggest man in the country."

He temptingly offered to reveal the Mob's most closely guarded secrets, to expose everyone from the top-echelon mobsters who were in bed with powerful politicos to the cutthroats who did the dirty work on the streets.

What did Reles want in return? A guarantee that he wouldn't be prosecuted for *any* of his crimes.

"I want to walk out clean," he declared.

Turkus was astounded at Reles's brazen demand that he be "entirely excused by society for committing over a dozen murders." On top of that, Reles wanted round-the-clock, heavily armed guards to protect him and his family from his former associates. He was all too familiar with the

Mob's steely resolve to rub out informers: "You don't know those bastards like I do," he shuddered. "Anywhere in the world they'd find me, if I was on the outside. Anywhere in the world—and they'd knock me off!"

O'Dwyer and Turkus left the room to confer, but there was really nothing for them to discuss. The ugly truth was that without Reles, the DA could never hope to make good on his vow to smash the Mob in Brooklyn. There was also the matter of O'Dwyer's political aspirations. He'd hoped to use the DA's office as a springboard to the mayoralty of New York City—and, perhaps, higher offices beyond that. He could kiss those dreams good-bye if his vaunted showdown with the underworld fizzled out.

In the end, O'Dwyer reluctantly agreed to Reles's demands. It was bitter medicine, but Turkus later called the agreement "the most valuable deal the Law ever made." And O'Dwyer would laud Reles as "the most effective informer in the annals of criminal justice." Neither man was exaggerating.

■■■

Why did Reles betray the Mob?

"Every one of those guys wanted to talk, only I beat them to the bandwagon" was his initial explanation. But the truth is that none of his cohorts tried to squeal so early in the game. It took weeks of pressure to make Dukey and Pretty crack. And Buggsy Goldstein, who was facing the possibility of the death penalty for the murder of Red Alpert, remained mum. Reles later changed his story, giving two altruistic reasons for squealing: "I was disgusted with the way I was living, the killing and all that. And the new baby was coming." These motives were laughable. Reles having a crisis of conscience over his way of life? He'd never shown any signs of even *having* a conscience. Reles wanted to be an exemplary dad? Where was that desire when his *first* child was born years earlier? Not surprisingly, few people bought Reles's self-serving explanations. Most saw him for what he was: a rat abandoning a sinking ship as fast as his feet would carry him.

■■■

Blessed with near-total recall—"He had the most amazing memory I have ever encountered," Burton Turkus commented—Reles's electrifying recital of Mob secrets lasted twelve straight days; a group of stenographers had to work in shifts to keep up with his chattering tongue.

How much damage did Reles do to the Mob? It was incalculable. Perhaps his most enduring contribution was that he confirmed what many in law enforcement had long suspected but had never been able to prove: that the Mob was "a nation-wide, highly organized business which operates major rackets from coast to coast, trains its personnel, has its own code of conduct, and kills on contract." Some top crime fighters, particularly FBI director J. Edgar Hoover, had dismissed the notion that there even was such an entity as organized crime. The Mob had been delighted that Hoover wasted his agency's resources chasing after two-bit crooks like John Dillinger, "Pretty Boy" Floyd, and "Baby Face" Nelson; the distraction had given the Mob precious time and freedom to entrench itself in the American economy.

On a practical level, Reles fingered the top organized crime figures in New York, New Jersey, Chicago, Detroit, Cleveland, Los Angeles, and other major metropolitan areas. He provided homicide detectives

O'Dwyer greets Reles upon his return from a grand jury appearance in California. [Corbis]

across the nation with rock-solid leads on dozens of unsolved Mob murders. And he named dozens of politicos whose palms were greased to keep the dirty money rolling in.

When he turned his attention to Brooklyn, Reles pursued a no-holds-barred policy against those who'd shared the gangster life with him. He held nothing back, delivering the goods to O'Dwyer and Turkus the same way he'd done for Lepke and Anastasia. The information he passed on to Brooklyn detectives enabled them to close the books on *eighty-five* murders. According to Turkus, who conducted the initial debriefings, Reles "rattled off names, places, facts, data of one manslaughter after another, days on end, without once messing up. He recalled not only the personnel involved, but decent people who had an unwitting part in some angle of the crime. He pointed out a cigar stand where a man happened to be standing when murderers went by in flight. [That information] provided a witness who placed the killers near the scene of the crime. He mentioned a filling station where the attendant sold a can of gasoline that had been used to burn up a body. The attendant proved [to be] a vital link of evidence against the cremators."

Reles also filled in crucial gaps in underworld history. The slaying of Dutch Schultz and three of his men at a New Jersey eatery in 1935 had been the subject of endless speculation in law enforcement circles.

"For five years the possible motives [for Schultz's murder] advanced had almost outnumbered the suspects," Turkus admitted. Only after Reles began singing "did the startling motive for the quadruple blood bath come out for the first time anywhere, except in the innermost sanctums of crime."

Schultz (born Arthur Flegenheimer in 1902) was one of the most colorful and psychopathic gangland characters of his era. He rose to prominence in the late 1920s by muscling in on highly profitable ventures like controlling beer distribution in the Bronx and running the numbers racket in Harlem. His abrasiveness rubbed other mobsters the wrong way, and he often found himself at violent odds with them.

On the night of October 23, 1935, the Dutchman was meeting with three aides-de-camp in a back room at the Palace Chop House in

Newark. Just as Schultz made a beeline for the restroom, two men calmly entered the joint. Mendy Weiss, one of Lepke's top hatchet men, covered the few patrons at the bar with a sawed-off shotgun while Charles "the Bug" Workman, a freelance hit man, cut down the trio at the back table before they knew what had hit them. Realizing that the Dutchman was not among them, Workman burst into the restroom and spotted his target at one of the urinals. He mortally wounded Schultz and, after rifling through the dying man's pockets for any bonus loot, fled the scene.

What was the "startling motive" Reles confided to Burton Turkus for the quadruple homicide? It was to save the life of the Mob's chief nemesis, Special Prosecutor Thomas E. Dewey!

Reles explained that Dewey had been making life difficult for the Dutchman by prying into Schultz's control of the numbers racket in Harlem. The daft Schultz's way out of his predicament was simply to whack Dewey: No prosecutor, no problem. At a meeting in New York City of Mob kingpins—including Lepke, Anastasia, and Charles "Lucky" Luciano—Schultz's plan was rejected with extreme prejudice. The proposed hit would surely backfire, most of the mobsters argued, resulting in a torrent of prosecutions the likes of which the country had never seen; the whole structure of organized crime would be shattered beyond repair. But Schultz was indignant with the decision of his peers. Bitterly, he announced that he would go it alone. With that, he stormed out of the meeting.

The ad hoc committee now had another major decision to make: What should be done to prevent Schultz from carrying out his threat? The slaughter at the Palace Chop House, Reles explained, was their answer.

Reles continued his morbid history lesson with the 1939 death of Peter Panto, the valiant young longshoreman who dared to challenge Albert Anastasia's dominance of the waterfront. While it had always been assumed that Panto had been murdered, his killers were never identified, and his body was never found. Reles changed all that. He identified Mendy Weiss, Lepke's ox-like enforcer and veteran of the Dutch Schultz hit, as the fiend who'd choked the life out of Panto with his bare hands. "Mendy strangled him as a favor for Albert," Reles told investigators. In the wake of the murder, Weiss had momentarily let his guard down: "Gee, I hated to take that kid," he confided to Reles. But Weiss quickly got ahold of himself. "I had to do it for Albert, because Albert has been good to me."

According to Reles, the body of the charismatic dockworker who might have changed labor history had been buried like so much garbage in a chicken farm in Lyndhurst, New Jersey.

"I think there's six or eight stiffs planted there," Reles added. He sketched out a map showing the presumed location of Panto's remains. Armed with spades and a steam shovel, workmen dug for close to three weeks without finding anything. Then, on January 29, 1941, they uncovered a six-hundred-pound block of frozen earth and quicklime; as the heavy mass was being moved, "chunks of the frozen lime broke off, disclosing part of the skeleton and ragged pieces of clothing." The remains were taken to the morgue, where a positive ID was later made. Even hardened lawmen were moved by the sorrow and the pity of Panto's wretched end.

PART II

THE CORPSE
ON
CONEY ISLAND

No one was safe from Abe Reles's poison arrows—not even the once untouchable Lepke. Reles spilled his guts about the shakedowns, vicious beatings, and murders the crime boss employed to build and maintain control of his empire. He boasted about how he kept Lepke, then the most hunted man in the world, hidden away for two years. (And he cheerfully turned in those who'd helped him conceal Lepke so that the feds could charge them with harboring a fugitive.) For Reles, though, the pièce de résistance was his proud retelling of how he'd helped Lepke orchestrate the slaughter of potential informers.

One of Reles's most sensational claims was that he could pin a first-degree murder charge on Albert Anastasia, Brooklyn's Lord High Executioner. The case involved Morris Diamond, the Teamster official who was bumped off in 1939 as part of Lepke's purge. Reles claimed to have overheard a planning session for the Diamond murder during a visit to Anastasia's home on Ocean Parkway in Brooklyn. "I came over to talk to Albert about our bookmaking business, and these two guys are sitting there," Reles recalled. "They are discussing a Morris Diamond matter." Reles identified the two guys as Mendy Weiss and Charles Workman.

As Reles eavesdropped, Anastasia gently scolded Weiss for a delay in whacking Morris Diamond. "Everything is ready, and you still haven't told us where the bum lives," he groused, according to Reles. "I'm working on it, Albert," Weiss answered. "As soon as I get it, I'll give it to you." To which Anastasia responded: "When I get it, we will take care of him."

Anastasia had made a dreadful mistake by allowing Reles to overhear his words. If he were ever to be tried for the Diamond murder, then Reles—who wasn't involved in the hit but who'd listened in on the planning session for it—would be eligible to give the non-accomplice testimony required by New York law. Angelo Catalano, who drove the getaway car (and who, like Reles, had become a material witness for the state), would give the accomplice testimony. A conviction would almost surely send Anastasia to the electric chair, making him the first Mob boss ever to be legally executed by court order in the United States.

When word reached Anastasia that Reles was squealing about the murder of Diamond, he and two of his top hit men, Dandy Jack Parisi—who actually shot Diamond—and Tony Romeo, quickly dropped out of sight.

■■■

Reles's revelations set off a media firestorm. The *New York Times* struggled to keep up with the daily slew of disclosures ("Two More Slayings Are Solved as Drive on Syndicate Takes On Added Momentum," "O'Dwyer Plans New Actions Against Racketeer in Slaying of Dewey Witness," "Lepke Aide, Long Missing, Is Found Slain"). In April 1940, shortly after Reles began singing, *Life* magazine carried a lurid feature spread that called his revelations "a horror tale, bigger and more odious" than anything its readers could imagine. Several grisly crime scene photos (including the trussed-up, charred body of Puggy Feinstein) and a gallery of mug shots were splashed across the pages. Though *Life* referred to the ugly affair in Brooklyn as "Murder, Inc.," that enduring sobriquet—a stark reference to the Combination's cool and efficient way of carrying out contract murders—was actually coined by Harry Feeney, crime reporter for the *New York World-Telegram*.

As Reles had predicted, O'Dwyer became the man of the hour. Philanthropist Harry Guggenheim, head of the Citizens Committee on the Control of Crime, praised the DA for "doing a striking job as prosecutor," adding that "what has been told makes as fantastic a tale of the ways and works of organized crime as we have ever heard." The media joined in the chorus of praise. The *New York Times* wrote glowingly that O'Dwyer had been "cutting away at the poisoned tissue" of the underworld since taking office, and it now appeared that "the operation would be a success." *Life* asserted that O'Dwyer had given America "its most startling crime story of the century." The magazine lamented that the war in Europe had "deprived [the Murder, Inc., affair] of the attention to which in normal times it would be entitled."

■■■

Away from the public eye, there were troubling signs that O'Dwyer was not the dedicated crusader against evil the press made him out to be. Indeed, some of his actions, had they become generally known, surely would have damaged his heroic image. For example, John Harlan Amen, still serving out his appointment as special prosecutor investigating political corruption in Brooklyn, discovered that the longshoremen's unions were serving as pipelines for the graft being paid to elected officials. In March 1940, he subpoenaed the financial records of the unions controlled by the six Camarda brothers (all of whom were lieutenants of Albert Anastasia) in the hope of documenting the money trail. The Camardas decided to fight the subpoena. Curiously, out of all the lawyers in New York City, they hired Paul O'Dwyer, brother of the Brooklyn DA. The case went all the way to the Supreme Court, where the Camardas lost.

Then, out of the blue, DA O'Dwyer announced that he was launching his own drive to rid the waterfront of Mob infestation. He proceeded to seize the Camardas' financial records—just minutes before Amen's men arrived to do the same thing. That was the beginning and the end of O'Dwyer's drive to clean up the docks; there were no further investigations, no indictments, no arrests. At first, O'Dwyer explained that the seized records had turned out to be fakes—the originals having been burned by the Camardas—so that it would be impossible to prosecute the unions. Later, he claimed (with a straight face) that prosecutions weren't necessary because the Camardas had promised to police themselves! O'Dwyer's inability to give a coherent explanation for failing to act wasn't an isolated incident: It was a harbinger of future situations where he would offer lame, sometimes laughable, excuses whenever his actions—or his inaction—attracted concern.

Truth be told, O'Dwyer reaped a huge reward from ignoring the insidious link between the waterfront and crooked politicians. He was able to devote virtually all of his time to Murder, Inc., a scandal with infinitely greater public appeal. The DA was nobody's fool; he understood "that a man who successfully prosecuted those heartless killers could get himself the kind of publicity that might lead directly to City

Hall." And it was no secret that Bill O'Dwyer had his sights on becoming the mayor of New York City.

■■■

Several of Reles's partners in crime—among them Seymour "Blue Jaw" Magoon, Sholem Bernstein, Mickey Sycoff, and, most unexpectedly, Lepke's top lieutenant Allie Tannenbaum—were soon pounding feverishly on O'Dwyer's door. Their closeness to Reles had tainted them in the eyes of the Mob's big shots; they'd become marked men living in fear of a fatal dose of lead. So each man cut a deal with the DA to become a "canary," as the press snidely referred to gangsters who decided to "sing." Reles was far and away the prize canary, but his true worth had yet to be tested where it really mattered: in the courtroom. If juries didn't believe the stories this miscreant had to tell, then the game would be over.

Reles passed his first test with flying colors. In May 1940, Harry Maione and Frank Abbandando were tried for the 1937 killing of George "Whitey" Rudnick, the suspected snitch who was stabbed and hacked to death in a Brooklyn garage. The day Reles was scheduled to testify, every spectator, including members of the press, was searched for weapons before being allowed to enter the courtroom. Police officials lined the walls, many refusing to believe that their old nemesis would rat out the Mob until they saw and heard it for themselves. When everyone was finally seated, Reles was escorted in. Considerably heavier than when he'd been taken into protective custody, he was dressed in a gray suit, a red tie, and a white shirt with long pointed collars that stuck out over his suit coat lapels. Although he was clean-shaven, a dark beard shadowed his face. As Reles walked to the witness stand flanked by two detectives who never left his side, his eyes nervously scanned the packed courtroom.

As the trial got under way, a reporter marveled at how Reles testified "with the utmost ease, spinning out an account of crime probably unparalleled in the annals of modern gangland history." For close to four hours, Burton Turkus guided his witness through his direct examination; Reles described "murder after murder in a somewhat similar fashion, occasionally injecting anecdotes with a broad, slapstick humor that brought chuckles to the spellbound spectators." Not everyone was amused. On the day Reles described Rudnick's gory murder, the judge adjourned the trial early because he "needed a rest."

Reles was caught off-guard only once. When asked on cross-examination if his testimony was "a violation of the same code of silence that had led him to order the murder of others," his perpetual smirk faded. He shifted uneasily in the witness chair, then answered sheepishly: "Well, it's not exactly the same thing."

Defendant Maione could sense that Reles was connecting with the jury. His rage at being sold out by his former partner grew by the minute. One day, as Reles was leaving the courtroom, Maione suddenly lunged at him. "You stool pigeon son of a bitch!" he shrieked, his eyes almost bursting from their sockets. "I'm gonna kill you! I'm gonna tear your throat out!" Unscathed, Reles was hustled out by his bodyguards; Maione was restrained after a brief struggle. In the end, Reles's poison had its effect: Maione and Abbandando were convicted of first-degree murder and sentenced to death. The two went to the electric chair on February 19, 1942.

Martin Goldstein and Harry Strauss, the next targets in O'Dwyer's shooting gallery, were tried in September 1940 for the strangulation murder of Puggy Feinstein in 1939. This time around, Reles was noticeably uncomfortable on the witness stand; Goldstein and Strauss had been his first allies in the Brownsville power grab a decade earlier. During his time on the stand, he avoided making eye contact with the pair. Yet his testimony was devastating. He gave a gut-wrenching account of how Puggy was strangled, and even gave a demonstration of the sadistic "rope-job" used on the victim. (In an eerie coincidence, the bells of a local church began pealing at noon, the very moment he described Puggy's last breath.) Reles's cool composure under heated cross-examination sealed the fate of his old buddies: The jury returned guilty verdicts against both men, and they were also sentenced to death.

As Goldstein boarded a train for the one-way ride to Sing Sing, he told reporters: "Just tell that rat Reles I'll be waiting for him. Maybe it'll be in Hell; I don't know. But I'll be waiting." Strauss's parting words were more visceral: "I just wanted to sink my tooth into his jugular vein. I didn't worry about the chair, if I could just tear his throat out first." The death sentence for both men was carried out on June 12, 1941.

■■■

And so the first round of Murder, Inc., trials ended with the four cofounders of the Combination headed to the death house. If the bosses of organized crime across the country had at first been in a state of disbelief over Reles's betrayal, they'd received a collective bucket of ice water in the face: This was really happening. Consumed with rage, they no longer spoke the name Reles; they spat it out. They knew it was only a matter of time before the rat sent *them* up the river—or worse, to the electric chair. As long as Reles remained alive, their fates hung in the balance. Something had to be done. Reles, for his part, had been certain that the bosses would react like cornered animals when their way of life was threatened. He was right.

Benjamin "Bugsy" Siegel. [Corbis]

District Attorney O'Dwyer received information that Benjamin "Bugsy" Siegel, the thirty-four-year-old crime boss of Southern California (best known as the founder of modern Las Vegas), had been chosen by his peers to plot Reles's assassination. The DA also learned that Siegel planned to use hit men from outside New York City in order to confuse local authorities who would be unfamiliar with the potential killers.

O'Dwyer reacted to the news by talking tough. "These men are here . . . to shoot down those who stand in the way," he told reporters. "They won't get far in Brooklyn. Siegel is here because the leaders of the Brooklyn Mob, the top men who should have taken over, have fled to cover. Siegel will try to restore order, to calm nerves, to guide things until the 'heat' is off. He will be a field director [who will] mark out those who must go." The DA assured his listeners that "additional guards had been placed over all witnesses and informers in the inquiry into the Brooklyn murder ring."

Previously classified FBI reports (obtained by the author under the Freedom of Information Act) reveal that despite his tough talk, O'Dwyer did fear losing Reles to a Mob bullet. When Reles was slated to fly to California in May 1941 for a grand jury appearance, O'Dwyer asked the FBI to stake out the airport in Chicago where the plane was scheduled to make a stopover, to determine "if there is any indication of activity on the part of any individuals to kill Reles when the plane lands." The FBI agreed that "an attempt may be made to 'get' Reles inasmuch as fourteen or fifteen men can be tried and convicted on his testimony for murder." Agents were sent to the airport to look out for trouble. They later reported that Reles and his three bodyguards wisely stayed out of harm's way by remaining in a remote part of the airfield.

Another previously classified FBI report shows that when Reles and Albert Tannenbaum were slated to testify before a New Jersey grand jury about the 1935 murder of mobster Dutch Schultz, O'Dwyer tried desperately to keep the actual date of their appearance secret because "an attempt might be made to assassinate Reles and Tannenbaum while en route" to the session. When the local prosecutor in New Jersey refused to oblige, O'Dwyer took the unusual step of asking the governor of the state to pressure the prosecutor into cooperating. Ultimately, O'Dwyer was successful in keeping the date under wraps.

The FBI took an active role in trying to keep Reles alive, passing along to O'Dwyer whatever tidbits it gleaned from confidential informants about Mob plots to kill Reles. At one point, the FBI learned that someone was tipping off Siegel's hit men that the DA's investigators were on their trail. At a meeting at the FBI's New York City office on

April 2, 1941, the surprising identity of the tipster was revealed:

> O'Dwyer was informed that in connection with the killers that
> were imported to New York City, that the contact was made at
> the Piccadilly Hotel, located at 227 West 45th Street, to com-
> plete the arrangements; that there are four mobsters who
> occupy four different suites of rooms at this hotel, namely an
> individual known by the name of [name redacted], another
> known by the alias of [name redacted] from Chicago, and
> [name redacted] of Newark, New Jersey. The name of the fourth
> individual is not known. Recently several of O'Dwyer's detec-
> tives conducted a discreet inquiry at the Piccadilly Hotel, as a
> result of which the house detective attached to that hotel com-
> municated with the above mentioned individuals, advising them
> that they were "hot" and to cool off until the detectives departed.
> [Name of confidential informant redacted] recently made the
> statement that the Mob is pretty well-fixed at the Piccadilly
> Hotel, inasmuch as they have on the payroll [name of house
> detective redacted], for the sum of $50.00 a week, and because
> of this remuneration, these mobsters are informed whenever any
> checking is done of them at this hotel.

Reles himself confided his fears about Mob vengeance to an FBI
agent he ran into at O'Dwyer's office:

> Reles made the statement to Special Agent [name redacted]
> asking when the Government was going to take him into cus-
> tody for safekeeping. He was advised that the Bureau was not
> intending to do this and was asked whether or not he was in a
> comfortable environment and being taken good care of by
> O'Dwyer. Reles stated that he was but he is getting a bit nervous
> lately, inasmuch as there are some strange individuals who are
> spotting him and Tannenbaum as they go and come from
> O'Dwyer's office. This information by Reles apparently checks
> with that given by [name of confidential informant redacted]

that two killers are here from the West Coast to take care of the squealer.

Several plots against Reles's life were only narrowly foiled. One called for him to be ambushed as he was being driven to the courthouse; the hit team would stage a traffic jam to trap the car in which the turncoat was riding. But authorities got wind of the plan, and Reles was transported in an armored car instead. Another scheme involved assassins with high-powered rifles who planned to cut down Reles as he was leaving the courthouse. The hit men, however, were never able to get off a clear shot because of the crowd of cops and reporters who surrounded Reles. Despite these setbacks, the Mob continued trying to assassinate Reles.

■■■

Early in the Murder, Inc., probe, O'Dwyer decided that the Mob turncoats wouldn't be housed behind bars; it was a given that the underworld could reach inside prison walls to snuff out a rat. "They'll get me if I'm in the clink," Reles told the DA. "They'll figure out a way to poison me or something." (There was no official witness protection program at the time, so each law enforcement jurisdiction was responsible for safeguarding its informers.) At first, O'Dwyer kept Abe Reles, Allie Tannenbaum, Sholem Bernstein, and Mickey Sycoff in protective custody at the Bossert Hotel in downtown Brooklyn. But security at the busy site proved difficult to manage, so in the fall of 1940 the four canaries were transferred to the isolated Half Moon Hotel on Coney Island.

Located at West 29th Street and the Boardwalk, the Half Moon was a Coney Island landmark. It was erected at the site where the English explorer Henry Hudson, sailing aboard the *Half Moon*, was said to have made landfall in the early seventeenth century. The four-hundred-room Spanish Colonial–style building had two eleven-story wings; the sixteen-story center section was topped off with a massive gold dome. The lavish interior was festooned with marble busts of Henry Hudson and hand-painted murals of exotic seaports. The nautical theme continued in the Isabella Dining Room and the Galleon Grille. The Grand Ballroom was home to the Half Moon Orchestra, which performed live radio broadcasts of dance music. When the hotel opened in 1927, the hope was that it might reverse the area's declining fortunes, but the renaissance never happened. By 1940, the Half Moon, like Coney Island itself, was but a ghost of its former glory.

The decision to relocate Reles and his three colleagues to the Half Moon Hotel was made by Captain Frank Bals of the NYPD, the forty-nine-year-old head of O'Dwyer's Special Investigations Squad. After canvassing several hotels, Bals found that the Half Moon was eager to have the DA's business. Paul Fulton, the manager of the hotel, agreed to the remodeling that would be needed to house Reles and company. A suite of ten rooms was created by sealing off the entire east wing of the sixth floor with a large, bulletproof steel door. This door, which was equipped with a large peephole, was the only entrance and exit to the suite. In addition to a series of locks, the door could be barricaded from inside by placing a wooden bar into metal brackets set in the door frame. One wag in the press dubbed the fortress-like lair Captain Bals created as "the squealers' suite," and the name caught on.

The Half Moon Hotel, Coney Island.
[Curt Teich Postcard Archives / Lake County (IL) Museum]

Three shifts of NYPD cops, five men per shift, guarded Reles and his three fellow snitches in the squealers' suite. Each shift was on duty for twenty-four hours—beginning at 10:00 a.m. one day and ending at 10:00 a.m. the next—then had forty-eight hours off. Uniformed cops also guarded the entrances to the hotel. Sergeant Elwood Divver, Captain Bals's deputy, was the direct supervisor of the guards. It's important to note that the security personnel enjoyed a great deal of autonomy: The guards were members of Bals's special squad, and they reported solely to the captain. Bals, in turn, answered only to O'Dwyer; in fact, he took the job with the understanding that he wouldn't have to report to his superiors in the NYPD.

The ten rooms of the squealers' suite, numbered 619 through 628, ran along a central corridor. Room 620, nearest to the steel door, was used as a command post by the guards. The only telephone in the suite was in room 620.

Abe Reles lived alone in room 623, toward the southern end of the suite, on the east side of the corridor.

Sholem Bernstein occupied room 622, next door to Reles. The dark-skinned, thirty-one-year-old Bernstein, also known as "Sol," had been Murder, Inc.'s, car thief extraordinaire, stealing vehicles

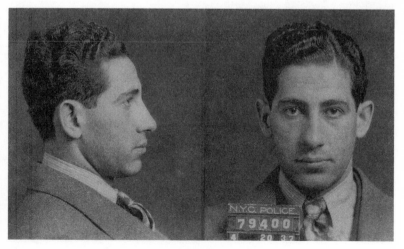

Sholem Bernstein. [NYC Municipal Archives]

used as getaway cars. Occasionally, Bernstein drove the getaway car, too: He was the wheelman in the murder of Joseph Rosen in 1936, and was involved in the 1938 murder of Hyman Yuran, another victim of Lepke's purge.

Allie Tannenbaum and Mickey Sycoff shared room 626, across the hall from Reles, on the west side of the corridor. Unlike his Murder, Inc., mates, the thirty-five-year-old Tannenbaum was not a native New Yorker. Born in the coal country of Nanticoke, Pennsylvania, he and his family had moved to Brooklyn when he was a baby. Allie Tannenbaum's entrée into the Mob was unique. As a teenager, he worked at a resort his dad owned in the Catskills. One summer, a bunch of Lepke's goons who were staying at the resort took a liking to the hardworking kid; Allie, in turn, was seduced by their devil-may-care demeanor. Soon he'd joined them in smacking around union workers, breaking strikes, and committing other acts of mayhem. Tannenbaum would eventually become the chief suspect in at least seven murders, but his thin, sad face always made him seem like a timid soul on the verge of bursting into tears.

Tannenbaum was the second most important canary in O'Dwyer's aviary. He was the only non-accomplice who could link Lepke to the

Albert Tannenbaum. [NYC Municipal Archives]

murder of Joseph Rosen. Tannenbaum had been present in Lepke's office when the boss said he would "take care" of Rosen, and again later when Mendy Weiss, one of the killers, reported back to Lepke that the hit had gone as planned. On the strength of Tannenbaum's statements, O'Dwyer obtained murder indictments against Lepke, Weiss, and Louis Capone. Excited by the prospect of ridding society of Lepke once and for all, the feds turned him and his two loyal deputies over to the Brooklyn DA to stand trial for the Rosen murder.

As he sat in the slammer awaiting his day in court, Lepke must have wondered how his instincts had failed him so miserably. First he'd allowed himself to be tricked into surrendering to the feds in 1939. Now he faced the electric chair because one of his most trusted lieutenants— someone he never gave the slightest thought to bumping off during the infamous purge—had betrayed him.

Meyer "Mickey" Sycoff, Tannenbaum's roommate, was thirty-three years old. He'd been one of Reles's most successful loan sharks. Though his rap sheet listed only minor arrests for robbery and vagrancy, the burly Sycoff was no stranger to violence. He was a hothead who resorted to vicious beatings if one of his customers was late in repaying a juice loan. And Sycoff didn't shy away from being an accomplice to

Mickey Sycoff. [NYC Municipal Archives]

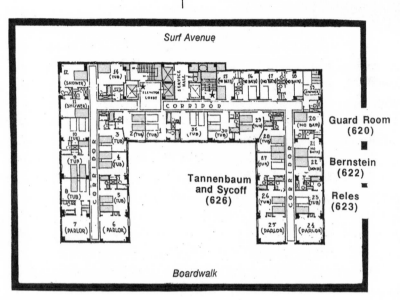

Sixth floor of the Half Moon Hotel. Squealers' suite, showing informers' rooms, at right. [NYC Municipal Archives]

murder, either: He lent a hand in the slayings of mobsters Joey Amberg (1935), Solomon Goldstein (1936), and Abraham Friedman (1939).

After inspecting the elaborate security arrangements at the Half Moon Hotel, Burton Turkus declared that Reles and his fellow snitches were being guarded "like the gold pile at Fort Knox." Then, on the morning of November 12, 1941, Turkus received a phone call from Harry Feeney, the crime reporter who'd coined the term Murder, Inc. "Hey Burt," Feeney said breathlessly, "Reles just went out the window!"

As Captain Frank Bals sped to the Half Moon Hotel on the early morning of November 12, 1941, he knew that his life was about to become a nightmare. *There's going to be hell to pay for losing Reles,* he thought. *The papers will have a field day with the story, internal affairs will be all over my ass, and our esteemed mayor, who never trusted the Brooklyn DA's office, will be shooting off his big mouth for weeks. Worst of all, though, is that I've let Bill O'Dwyer down. Bill had asked me for one simple thing: "Don't let anything happen to Reles." So how did I show Bill that I could handle the job, that I was more than just an old pal from the force? By letting Reles do a swan dive right under the noses of the men I picked to watch him like a hawk day and night!*

By the time he reached the Half Moon at around 7:30 a.m., Bals had worked himself into a fury. Once inside the squealers' suite, his pent-up rage at the guards exploded. "What the hell happened?" he bellowed. "Did you all fall asleep?"

The men didn't say a word.

What the hell is the matter with these dumb bastards? Bals wondered. *Standing around like potted plants . . . Don't they realize what a world of trouble they're in?* He turned and stormed down the hall to Reles's room, where a portable radio was still playing, the bed was disheveled, and a bedspread was strewn across the floor. Bals went to the window and gazed down at the sorry sight of Reles's body on the kitchen extension roof fifty-two feet below. *Sonofabitch,* he muttered under his breath. *Sonofabitch.* He returned to the front of the suite and confronted the guards again. "You better get your stories straight!" he barked. It sounded like part warning, part threat.

Determined to keep a lid on news of the debacle for as long as possible, Bals telephoned the dispatcher at the station house with orders that anyone—reporters, cops, citizens—who asked about the body at the Half Moon should be told that it was that of "an unknown DOA."

Next, Bals phoned Lieutenant Joseph Donovan of the Brooklyn Homicide Squad. He asked Donovan to send a crime scene processing team to the Half Moon. *And ask the Old Man to drop by*, Bals added, trying to make it sound like an afterthought. Donovan was astonished: Bals wanted the Old Man there? This had to be something big. He pressed for details and, reluctantly, the captain confided that Reles was dead. But Bals begged Donovan to keep the news under his hat to avoid tipping off the reporters who hung around the station house waiting for a scoop. Donovan agreed—but he also decided that he didn't want to sit around while all the excitement was going on so close by. So he rounded up a crime scene team—Detectives William Cush and Charles Celano, photographer Harold O'Neil, and stenographer John Burns— and was at the Half Moon by 8:00 a.m.

A few minutes later, the Old Man arrived. Captain John J. McGowan, the fifty-five-year-old head of the Brooklyn Homicide Squad, strode confidently into the suite and launched the official investigation into the death of Abe Reles.

■■■

John J. McGowan was larger than life. His brothers in blue relished trading stories about his two-fisted exploits. There was the time he beat a murderer senseless after the creep aimed a pistol at him and pulled the trigger—incredibly, the gun misfired; the time he waged a one-man crusade to rid the streets of pedophiles, ignoring legal niceties in order to get the job done; and the time he personally closed the book on a string of killings near the waterfront by roughing up the prime suspect. But McGowan was more than just a cowboy. He pioneered the use of forensic science in police work, including a system for classifying knots that was widely used in the New York City Police Department. In one famous case, McGowan solved a vicious strangulation murder by matching the knot from the noose to a type used in the merchant marine. Sure enough, a former sailor later confessed to the homicide.

McGowan was considered a cop's cop: steady, dependable, a team player who would never do anything to embarrass the NYPD. Bill O'Dwyer was one of his biggest fans. They'd known each other since their days as beat cops. On the momentous day that Reles decided to squeal, it was John McGowan—along with Frank Bals—whom O'Dwyer chose for the high-risk job of safely transporting Reles from the Tombs jail to the DA's office; there were fears that the Mob would try to silence Reles before he could sing a note. Later on, when it came time to arrest the men Reles had fingered, O'Dwyer had put McGowan at the helm of the operation. With his old pal running the show, the DA felt certain that nobody would slip through the dragnet.

■■■

McGowan made no secret of the fact that he didn't give a rat's ass about the "victim" in this case. Star witness or no, Reles was the scum of the earth, and Brooklyn was well rid of him. Though McGowan silently cursed Bals for dragging him into this mess, he knew that Frank needed help cleaning it up. And there was Bill O'Dwyer to think of. *They're both good men,* the captain reasoned. *They shouldn't lose everything because of a no-account mutt like Reles.* With these thoughts in the back of his mind, McGowan wandered through the suite, firing observations at stenographer Burns and directing photographer O'Neil to take specific shots—like a view of the corpse from the window in Reles's room.

Reles's corpse as seen from window in his room (NYPD crime scene photo). [NYC Municipal Archives]

Meanwhile, Captain Bals was thinking about damage control. He realized that no one from the DA's office was present to look after O'Dwyer's interests. So he called Assistant DA Edward Heffernan, one of O'Dwyer's top aides. After telling him the shocking news, Bals offered to bring him to the hotel to pursue his own investigation; Heffernan agreed. As he waited outside his home for Bals to pick him up, Heffernan tried to come to grips with the fact that the Murder, Inc., probe had been dealt a devastating blow. With Reles gone, dozens of cases against mobsters would have to be tossed out. Worst of all, Albert Anastasia would never be held accountable for the slaying of Morris Diamond, as the case depended completely on Reles's testimony. Heffernan could almost sense Anastasia's sigh of relief blowing through Brooklyn.

Bals and Heffernan reached the Half Moon shortly after 9:00 a.m. Bals was mortified when he entered the squealers' suite and found it crawling with police brass. Word of Reles's death had quickly made its way through the NYPD grapevine, and any hope the captain had of bottling up the disastrous news was, like Reles himself, out the window. Heffernan was appalled from a prosecutor's point of view. Since no one knew whether this was a murder, a suicide, or an accident, the squealers' suite was considered a crime scene. Why hadn't Captain McGowan sealed it off? Why hadn't he stopped the curiosity seekers from poking around and possibly tainting vital evidence?

Heffernan was also surprised that Captain McGowan had yet to interrogate or even sequester the eight people—the three Murder, Inc., informers and five guards—who were in the suite when Reles went out the window. Until things were sorted out, they all had to be considered suspects. But instead of being interrogated, they were mingling with the throng of gawkers. Heffernan began to take charge. He phoned Frank Maguire, a stenographer with the DA's office, and told him to come to the hotel. He then rounded up the eight witnesses, along with Captain Bals and his deputy, Sergeant Elwood Divver, and ushered them into the large parlor room at the rear of the suite. The exodus caught the attention of McGowan, Detectives Celano and Cush, and several of the police brass, all of whom invited themselves to sit in on the interrogation.

Heffernan was right about getting witnesses on the record as soon as possible, but he went about it the wrong way. By questioning the witnesses within earshot of one another, he gave them the opportunity to concoct matching answers. As a seasoned prosecutor, Heffernan must have known better than to interrogate witnesses as a group. Why he did so anyway is a mystery.

Stenographer Frank Maguire arrived, and the questioning began. Heffernan asked Allie Tannenbaum and Mickey Sycoff, the squealers who shared a room across the hall from Reles, when they had last seen Reles alive. Tannenbaum said it was shortly before eleven o'clock the previous night, while Sycoff remembered seeing him shortly after midnight. Both men claimed they hadn't heard any unusual noises during the night; in fact, they had no idea anything was amiss until they heard a ruckus in the suite that morning. Tannenbaum, who was getting dressed at the time of the commotion, told Heffernan: "I opened up my door and I walked out and saw the detectives [*sic*] excited. I asked, 'What is the matter?' They said: 'Abe went out the window.'"

Tannenbaum and Sycoff reported that Reles's wife, Rose, had visited her husband the previous night. She was behind closed doors with him from about 7:00 p.m. until around 10:00 p.m.—an unusually long period compared with her previous visits. She looked irate when she finally emerged. Rose had left the suite quickly without saying a word to anyone. Tannenbaum grumbled to Heffernan that it was the first time "she never asked me how my family was." The stone-cold killer's sensitive feelings were still smarting from the snub.

Switching subjects, Heffernan asked if the guards (who were sitting a few feet away) had been doing their duty:

Q: What supervision do they have over you after you retire, do you know?

TANNENBAUM: Oh, yes, they come into the room . . .

Q: As far as you are concerned, you know that you were constantly under supervision during the course of the night?

TANNENBAUM: Yes, sir.

Sycoff seconded his roommate's answers:

Q: As far as your room is concerned, were you being watched all
   the time?
SYCOFF: As far as I know.
Q: When you are limiting it that way, I suppose you mean you
   don't know what happens when you sleep? But when you were
   awake, you knew that the detectives were watching you?
SYCOFF: Yes.
Q: And that is true of all of you, I assume?
SYCOFF: Yes.

Heffernan was curious as to why Reles didn't have a roommate.
Tannenbaum piped up that he, for one, "didn't even like being in the
same room" with Reles:

Q: Why was that?
TANNENBAUM: From what I seen [*sic*], I knew he was a real sick
   man. The man spit blood and he used to spit in his hand and
   cough in your face, and every time he would bring up a mouth
   full of blood, he would bring it around and show everybody.
   Then he would spit into a glass and wait until it got full until he
   got rid of it.
Q: The man had filthy habits?
TANNENBAUM: Yes, and I didn't like the idea.

Tannenbaum had never been troubled by the buckets of blood he'd
freely spilled as a professional killer, but Reles's filthy habits were too
much for him to bear. Reles coughed up blood because he suffered
from bronchiectasis, a chronic lung disease. In fact, it was only the
previous Sunday, November 9, that Reles had returned to the squealers' suite after being hospitalized for nine days with an attack of
bronchiectasis.

A patrolman interrupted the questioning with word that Dr.
Gregory Robillard, an assistant medical examiner, was waiting on the

extension roof for the green light to inspect the corpse. A large group—Heffernan, Bals, McGowan, Detectives Celano and Cush, photographer O'Neil, stenographer Burns, and at least six police brass—headed outside to observe Dr. Robillard's examination. Incredibly, the eight witnesses were left in the parlor room without supervision.

As the group gathered on the extension roof, Harold O'Neil prepared to photograph the corpse from several angles before Dr. Robillard began his work. It was standard procedure to document the appearance of the corpse before the medical examiner altered it. Captain McGowan had scrupulously followed this

The presumed trajectory of Reles's fatal fall. [Brooklyn Public Library, Brooklyn Collection]

procedure in scores of previous cases. But this time was different. McGowan waved off O'Neil and instructed Robillard to begin. O'Neil was mystified; Detectives Celano and Cush, among others, exchanged confused glances. But no one uttered a word in protest.

As Robillard began his work, McGowan hovered over him, dictating comments to stenographer Burns:

The coat is turned up on the left side, and there is a gray checkered cap in the left trouser pocket. The trousers in the middle seam are torn for a distance of about ten inches, as are the drawers (apparently from the force of the fall). On the shoes, particularly the left shoe, there is considerable scraping from the inner side to the outer side. This does not show up on the right foot with the exception of at the toe of the shoe.

Robillard rolled Reles onto his back and tore open his sweater and shirt. He checked the body for bullet or knife wounds, finding none. He also checked for blunt-force trauma but found no evidence of that, either. Reles's fatal injuries were not inconsistent with a fall, the doctor announced, but any definitive conclusions about cause of death would have to await the autopsy, which he planned to perform later that day. It was only now, after Robillard had completely changed the position and appearance of the body, that Captain McGowan allowed Harold O'Neil to take one photograph—and only one—of the corpse.

Captain Bals asked Robillard if he could estimate Reles's time of death. The doctor reckoned that based on the corpse's temperature, Reles had been dead for about three to four hours. He cautioned, however, that the chilly weather and brisk ocean breezes likely *accelerated* the cooling of the corpse, while Reles's jacket and sweater probably *slowed* it. As Robillard packed up his medical bag, he said that he would send for a morgue wagon to pick up the body.

McGowan ordered Patrolman Paul Johnston, who had been guarding

Reles's corpse after inspection by the medical examiner (NYPD crime scene photo). [NYC Municipal Archives]

the body, to search it. Johnston found a Waltham pocket watch with chain, $2.35 in cash, and a key to room 623 at the Half Moon Hotel. This last item made Captain Bals's blood boil. He'd forbidden the squealers from having room keys because a locked door would interfere with the periodic bed checks the guards were supposed to perform. Yet Reles had somehow gotten a key. Though he felt like throttling the guards, Bals kept their blatant disregard of his order to himself.

McGowan moved on to the bedsheets with the strip of wire attached to one end lying near the body. Once again, he mishandled the processing of the crime scene: Before Harold O'Neil had a chance to photograph this crucial piece of evidence, McGowan picked it up, took it to the hotel wall, and draped it over a window frame. He instructed O'Neil to take a single photo, then told Detectives Celano and Cush to measure the sheets and wire: The two sheets were about nine feet in length overall and the strip of wire, about four. McGowan began to suspect that this contraption was a makeshift rope that Reles had used in an escape attempt. The captain recalled seeing a radiator directly below the window in Reles's room, and it struck him as an ideal place for Reles to have tied one end of this makeshift rope.

McGowan and his entourage returned to Reles's room. The captain ordered Detectives Cush and Celano to inspect the radiator for any

The makeshift rope posed against the hotel wall (NYPD crime scene photo). [NYC Municipal Archives]

indication that the makeshift rope had been fastened there. They seemed to hit pay dirt right away. On the pipe connecting the top of the radiator to the steam valve, they noticed a small area where the paint had been scraped off, exposing the bare metal underneath.

As the detectives were pondering the possible significance of their find, Paul Fulton, the manager of the Half Moon Hotel, elbowed his way into Reles's room. Fulton—who was among the curiosity seekers milling around the squealers' suite—had apparently been doing some detective work of his own. He told McGowan that he'd just found "something strange" while looking in unit 523, the vacant room directly below Reles's. Fulton led the McGowan group down there and showed them that the half screen outside the window was raised to within six inches of the top, and the window latch was turned about a quarter of an inch. He was sure that the previous guests had left the screen *down* on the lower half of the window when they'd checked out a few days earlier. Obviously, he declared, someone had tampered with the screen and latch in an attempt to break into the room from the outside of the building. Harold O'Neil came forward to snap a picture of the window but McGowan stopped him. Celano and Cush offered to canvas the adjacent rooms to determine if anyone had heard Reles fiddling with the screen, but the captain said it wouldn't be necessary.

Captain McGowan had seen and heard enough.

Left: Reles's room on the morning of his death (NYPD crime scene photo). [NYC Municipal Archives]

Right: The window in Reles's room (photographed in 1951). [NYC Municipal Archives]

Chapter 8

A Fatal Misstep

Paul Fulton's discovery clinched a theory Captain McGowan had been formulating: Abe Reles was killed as the result of a bungled escape attempt. Reles's plan, McGowan explained to the assembled crowd, had been to get into Room 523, slink through the hotel to the ground floor, then make a break for freedom. At some point between bed checks (probably 6:45 a.m. to 7:15 a.m.), McGowan continued, Reles put his plan into motion. He secured the wire attached to one end of the makeshift rope to the radiator pipe, then dropped the two knotted bed-sheets out his window. The distance to Room 523 was about ten feet, so the thirteen-foot device would have done the trick. (It's unclear, however, how Reles could have been sure of its length.) Then, Reles had climbed down the sheets until he got his footing on the stone windowsill of room 523. He raised the screen and was in the process of turning the window latch when he lost his footing and slipped off the windowsill. His dangling weight caused the wire to pull free from the radiator pipe—scraping off some paint as it did—and Reles plunged to his death.

When McGowan finished his pitch, it was as if an oracle had pronounced its judgment. Everyone simply nodded in silent agreement.

Then they returned to the squealers' suite, where McGowan's escape-attempt theory was discussed in hushed tones. Upon hearing about the wire on the makeshift rope, one of Reles's guards retrieved "more of the insulated wire of the type found attached to the sheet lying alongside of the body" from a closet in the parlor room. He explained to McGowan that the hotel engineer had provided the wire to make antennas for the portable radios in the suite. These samples might have been useful to the investigation, but the captain didn't bother to keep a single one.

Meanwhile, Captain Bals suddenly realized that he hadn't yet notified Reles's wife that her husband was dead. It should have been a simple task, but Bals managed to bungle it royally. He phoned Detective John McCarthy, a member of the captain's Special Investigations

Squad, and instructed him to have Mrs. Reles brought to the Half Moon. McCarthy made the necessary arrangements, then went to the hotel prior to her arrival to observe what was going on. As he was milling around the squealers' suite and in Reles's room, McCarthy ran into an anxious Frank Bals. To McCarthy's surprise, the captain now wanted him to *prevent* Mrs. Reles from entering the hotel.

"Go out to the corner and meet Mrs. Reles," Bals commanded. "But don't tell her what happened. Take her down to my office."

McCarthy hurried down the corridor to the elevator bank—just as Mrs. Reles and her police bodyguards were emerging from one of the elevators. (To avoid arousing her suspicion, Mrs. Reles had been told that her husband wanted to see her before leaving town to testify at a trial in California.) McCarthy was able to intercept Mrs. Reles and her protectors and whisk them off to Bals's office more than ten miles away. Once there, he told her to wait for Captain Bals. For the next several hours, cops came in and out of Bals's office to leave paperwork on his desk, yet none of them told her the news.

At the Half Moon, Assistant DA Heffernan returned to the parlor room to resume his interrogations. The next witness was Sholem Bernstein, who lived in the room adjacent to Reles. Like Tannenbaum and Sycoff, Bernstein said he hadn't heard any unusual sounds during the night, and that he hadn't known anything was wrong until he heard the ruckus in the suite that morning. Although Bernstein couldn't recall anything unusual about Reles's recent behavior, he did notice that Reles had lost a lot of weight during his recent hospital stay and appeared "anemic." Lately, Reles had become convinced that his doctors were hiding the severity of his illness from him. "They won't tell me what's wrong," he'd whined to Bernstein.

Heffernan asked Bernstein if the guards were always on their toes:

Q: Now, during the course of the night, do you know whether the guards maintain a constant vigilance?
BERNSTEIN: Yes.
Q: Do you ever see any of them around at night?
BERNSTEIN: I know they are around.

Q: What supervision do the detectives maintain?
BERNSTEIN: They walk around.
Q: The doors [to the witnesses' rooms] are left open?
BERNSTEIN: Yes, sir.

Now the five guards—Detectives Victor Robbins, James Boyle, and John Moran, along with Patrolmen Harvey McLaughlin and Francesco Tempone—took their turn on the hot seat. Heffernan began by asking Robbins about his actions that morning:

Q: When did you first discover that Reles was not in his room?
ROBBINS: About ten after seven, between 7:00 and ten after seven this morning.
Q: And how did you find that out?
ROBBINS: I walked down the hall and looked into his room and saw the spread on the floor and the window open.
Q: Did you go into the room?
ROBBINS: I went into the room and looked out the window.
Q: And when you looked out the window, what did you see?
ROBBINS: I saw the body laying down on the roof.

It was a brazen lie. The truth was that Robbins didn't have a clue that Reles was missing until Paul Fulton, the hotel manager, phoned him about the body on the roof. Heffernan gave Robbins a chance to retract the lie, but the detective wouldn't budge:

Q: You had not been notified of [Reles] being down there before?
ROBBINS: No.

Patrolman McLaughlin came to Robbins's aid. "When Detective Robbins went downstairs," McLaughlin interjected, "the phone rang and somebody said there's a man on the roof. I said I know it. A man is on the way down." Heffernan didn't hide his suspicions:

Q: And that notification by phone came when the detective was
already downstairs?

McLaughlin: Yes, the detective was on the way. He was out the
door and on the way down.

Heffernan asked Detective Robbins when he'd last seen Reles
alive. Robbins said it was "about an hour or an hour and a half" before
seeing the corpse on the roof. Since Robbins claimed he saw the corpse
on the roof at around 7:00 a.m., then the last time he saw Reles alive
must have been *between 5:30 a.m. and 6:00 a.m.* But then Robbins
immediately contradicted himself:

Q: You say you went into his room this morning about 7:00 or
7:10. How long before that had you seen Reles?

Robbins: About 4:00 o'clock. He was in bed.

Q: And had you seen him between 4:00 and 7:00?

Robbins: *No, I hadn't seen him between 4:00 and 7:00.*

Heffernan turned to Detective Boyle, the senior man on duty. He
asked if Boyle had kept a close eye on Reles the previous night:

Q: How frequently had you visited his room during the night?

Boyle: Oh, quite often. I or one of the others here go up and
down this hall frequently, say every ten or fifteen minutes,
and go all through and look at the rooms and look at the men
in bed.

Q: In other words, I understand you to mean that the squad
always has one man up and around?

Boyle: That's right, there's always somebody up and around.

All of the guards insisted that they had made periodic checks of the
squealers throughout the night. Detective John Moran's answer was
typical:

Q: How frequently had you seen him [Reles] during the course
   of the night?
MORAN: Oh, I don't know, maybe ten times.
Q: Now, during the course of the night, do you know if the other
   detectives assigned with you had visited these rooms?
MORAN: Oh, yes, everybody takes a walk around.
Q: About how frequently?
MORAN: Oh, about every ten or fifteen minutes.

The guards also claimed they hadn't heard any unusual noises ema-
nating from Reles's room during the night—particularly the kind of
sounds that might have hinted Reles was putting together his
makeshift rope. Patrolman McLaughlin:

Q: Had you heard any disturbance or any noise in that room?
McLAUGHLIN: No, sir.
Q: You didn't hear any tearing sound or anything of that kind?
McLAUGHLIN: No.

Mindful of Captain McGowan's theory that Reles had been killed
while trying to escape, Heffernan asked if Reles ever showed signs of
wanting to flee. The answers were clearly not what McGowan wanted
to hear. Patrolman Tempone:

Q: Did he ever say or do anything that indicated he wanted to
   escape?
TEMPONE: No.

Detective Boyle:

Q: During the time that you have been on this assignment, had
   any of these witnesses ever given any indication that they
   were going to try to make an escape?
BOYLE: No, I never found anything like that.

Detective Moran:

> Q: Was there anything that would indicate to you that he was planning to escape?
> MORAN: No.

In fact, Moran added, Reles was so petrified of Mob revenge that he didn't even feel completely safe *inside* the squealers' suite: "He used to look for the guard or want him to be alongside of him for fear that somebody might get in and harm him," Moran explained.

Finally, Sergeant Divver and Captain Bals took center stage. When Heffernan asked about the caliber of security, Divver let it be known that he ran a tight ship:

> Q: Now when these witnesses retire for the night, does the detail of police officers retire too, or do they remain alert?
> DIVVER: Oh no, they are instructed to be on alert at all times, particularly at night.
> Q: And do you from time to time visit during the night to check up on them?
> DIVVER: Very frequently.
> Q: How about the supervision of these witnesses while they are asleep?
> DIVVER: They were instructed to comply with police regulations and visit them at regular intervals during the night to make sure that they were in bed.

Heffernan also asked Divver about the mental state of the squealers:

> Q: Had you ever had any indication relayed to you that any of these witnesses had tried to escape?
> DIVVER: No.

Captain Bals, who claimed that he had made frequent visits to the suite at different hours of the day and night, testified that everything ran like clockwork:

Q: How frequently did your men supervise or inspect the rooms in which these witnesses slept?

BALS: They were given instructions to guard the big door, that is, the entrance to this apartment [*sic*]; that when the witnesses went to bed, their doors were to be left open; that the men were to stay awake, and for that purpose the room where the detectives and the patrolmen are stationed has no beds in it, but there are a number of chairs; that they were to visit these witnesses while they were in bed at the smallest interval possible, 15 minutes or less to walk through [the suite]. From my supervision and from the reports I received from Sergeant Divver these instructions were strictly complied with.

Bals added that the supervision of the guards "was of the strictest [*sic*]," and that he had "transferred men right out of this detail the minute they did not live up to the rules and regulations laid down by myself and Sergeant Divver." Security procedures were scrupulously observed, Bals said, because he had "confidential information that the underworld had made plans to do bodily harm to these witnesses."

Divver and Bals were both gung-ho about McGowan's escape-attempt theory. But their answers to some of Heffernan's questions actually undercut the theory, and neither man seemed to realize it. Divver:

Q: Have you a theory, Sergeant, as to what caused Reles to go out [*sic*] today?

DIVVER: Well, I believe that he tried to escape.

Q: What makes you think that?

DIVVER: The condition of the bedclothes, and I know that the room directly underneath is vacant.

Q: How long has that [room] below Reles's been vacant?

DIVVER: That I don't know, but I know it has been vacant for some time.

Q: Do you know whether Reles would know that it was vacant?

DIVVER: Well, yes, he would know that.

Q: How would he know?

DIVVER: He or one of the men might have been discussing it, that is possible.

Q: But you do not know that definitely?

DIVVER: No, I don't know.

Bals enthusiastically pointed out that "the shiny surface" on the radiator pipe "would conclusively indicate that the wire had been wound around it and had been tied there, and due to the weight of the body, had slipped off there, making that part of the radiator shiny and taking the paint off." In the very next breath, however, he contradicted himself by saying that he didn't believe Reles would have had the guts to make a risky escape attempt:

Q: Was there anything in his attitude at any time indicative to you of a tendency on his part either towards suicide or escape?

BALS: Never. From my personal observation, Reles was more concerned about his well-being than anybody that I know of. He was more in fear of harm coming to him from the outside than doing anything to harm himself. As a matter of fact, my personal observation of him was this: I would say that I considered him so cowardly that he would never do any personal injury to himself. As a matter of fact, he thought too much of himself.

Fresh out of questions, Heffernan turned the witnesses over to McGowan. Despite a reputation as a tough and thorough interrogator, the captain didn't explore a single inch of new territory. In fact, he didn't even bother to question Tannenbaum, Bernstein, and Sycoff. The transcript of his interrogation is a mere nine double-spaced pages, while Heffernan's Q&A fills some sixty pages.

Outside the hotel, a pack of unruly reporters who'd gotten wind of Reles's death were loudly demanding answers. The police kept them at bay by setting up barricades at the hotel's entrances, but the situation was getting out of hand. Heffernan tossed the reporters a bone and issued a statement. But how much could he really say? After all, the investigation was just getting started. The hotel's guests, tenants, and employees had yet to be questioned. Reles's wife had yet to be asked about the stormy visit that Allie Tannenbaum said she'd had with her husband the night before. The physical evidence had yet to be analyzed. The autopsy had yet to be performed. The situation, then, seemed to call for some limited remarks. Surprisingly, Heffernan threw caution to the wind. After herding the reporters into the hotel ballroom, he gave a note-for-note recital of the escape-attempt theory—right down to Detective Robbins's lie about finding Reles's body:

> There are five guards working in [twenty-four-hour] shifts keeping a strict supervision over the material witnesses. After the witnesses go to bed, the doors to the rooms are opened. Reles was sleeping alone in Room 623. His door was open. The rooms in which these material witnesses are kept are visited at 15-minute intervals. Sometime between 7 a.m. and 7:10 a.m. Detective Victor Robbins went to Reles' room. He discovered Reles missing. Robbins looked out and saw a body on the extension roof. He rushed downstairs.
>
> It was discovered that two bedsheets were knotted together, one end of which was attached to about four feet of insulated wire, the end of the wire being wound around the piping of the radiator. This wire was brought to the room by the hotel engineer to fix a radio several months ago.
>
> It is our belief that Reles tried to swing into the room below, Room 523, recently vacated, in order to make his escape. The sheets were only long enough for him to reach the floor below. We discovered that both his shoes were scraped, which perhaps occurred when he stood on the window ledge and tried to open the window. He probably made a misstep and his weight (160 pounds) unwound the wire from the radiator and he fell to the deck.

The reporters shouted questions—*Why would Reles want to escape? How did he know the room under his was vacant?*—but Heffernan ignored them. He had to get on with the unpleasant duty of reporting on the debacle to his boss, DA O'Dwyer.

Heffernan gave the reporters the slip and hooked up with Captain Bals. They drove together to O'Dwyer's home. Heffernan walked the DA through the escape-attempt theory. O'Dwyer listened in silence. Amazingly, he didn't express any outrage that his star witness—the man who, among other things, had made him something akin to a national hero—was gone forever. He even instructed Heffernan not to continue his inquiry into Reles's death, preferring, he said, to leave the investigation to the police.

Did Heffernan happen to remind O'Dwyer that Reles's well-known fear of Mob vengeance flew in the face of the escape-attempt theory? Did he mention that one of the guards told a blatant lie about finding the body? Did Bals put in his two cents about the guards possibly being asleep when Reles fell to his death? We'll never know. The participants later claimed they couldn't recall much of what was said at the meeting.

It was now around noon. Back at the Half Moon, Captain McGowan made an extraordinary decision: He would wrap up his investigation without questioning any of the hotel's employees, guests, or tenants. Vital witnesses like William Nicholson, who first spotted Reles's corpse, and Paul Fulton, whose amateur detective work contributed to the escape-attempt theory, were never formally interviewed. Fred Wolfarth and George Govans, the hotel employees who heard a loud thud outside the hotel at around 4:30 a.m., were also ignored, as were the cops who'd guarded the hotel's entrances.

McGowan didn't perform any better with the physical evidence. He never had the windowsill in Reles's room inspected for any smears of insulation from the wire that was allegedly stretched over it. He never gave the makeshift rope to the crime lab so that it could be examined for traces of paint from the radiator pipe. He never had the pipe removed so that the lab could determine if paint had indeed been scraped off by the wire. He never had Reles's shoes tested to establish if the scrape marks were made by contact with the stone windowsill outside of Room 523. Shockingly, McGowan didn't submit even a single piece of evidence in the Reles case to the crime lab.

■■■

Dr. Gregory Robillard performed the autopsy that afternoon. His external examination of the body revealed pockmarks in the left side of the face caused by contact with the gravel roof. The tongue was protruding, and blood had trickled from the nose and mouth. There was an eighteen-inch tear in Reles's pants that extended from just below the front of the waistband "down across the base of the crotch into the left buttock." The doctor noted Reles's bizarre tattoos: on the right forearm, a "grotesque, dwarf-like female," and a bird with the inscriptions TRUE LOVE above and MOTHER below; on the left forearm, a "heart with two female heads."

After dissecting the body, Robillard discovered hemorrhaging in the left side of the head (although there was no evidence of any direct trauma to the skull or brain), rupturing of the liver and spleen, and blood in the abdominal cavity. The spinal cord was fractured between the fourth and fifth lumbar vertebrae. On the left side of the torso, the second and third ribs were fractured, and the twelfth rib had punctured the diaphragm.

The autopsy was not without controversy. Though it's standard procedure for the detectives on a case to attend the postmortem, no one from the Homicide Squad showed up. Nor did DA O'Dwyer bother to send a representative—even though these were the remains of his star witness. But according to a note Robillard scribbled on the autopsy report—"Withhold information by order of D.A."—someone in O'Dwyer's office tried to suppress the results. Did the order come from the DA himself? Was it given before the autopsy began, in an effort to muzzle Robillard in the event he found signs of foul play? The answer to both questions remains unknown.

Robillard concluded that the cause of death was a combination of factors: the fractured vertebrae, the ruptured liver and spleen, and the hemorrhaging in the abdominal cavity. He removed the brain, liver, kidneys, and stomach and sent them to the toxicology lab to be tested for drugs, alcohol, and poisons.

■■■

By late afternoon, Mrs. Reles was still waiting at Captain Bals's office. She'd practically given up hope that the captain would show up to explain why she'd been hustled down to the Half Moon Hotel, only to be diverted to his office. At long last, Bals appeared. He'd had a long day, and seeing Mrs. Reles reminded him that it wasn't over yet. When he finally delivered the bad news, she became inconsolable. "What have they done to him?" she wept. And then: "Who did it? Who did it?" Eventually, she calmed down enough to answer some of Bals's questions. Unfortunately, Bals kept no record of the conversation, and he later claimed that it was a complete blank in his memory.

■■■

At day's end, Detective Cush filed his first report on the case. He wrote that at some point "between 7:00 & 7:15 a.m." Reles "fell from a six [*sic*] story window when he tried to escape." Curiously, no mention was made of Reles's supposed effort to enter the room on the fifth floor—a crucial part of McGowan's escape-attempt theory. The slip-up was swiftly corrected: Cush immediately filed a second report in which he added that Reles had "lowered himself to the window of room #523" when his makeshift rope failed.

Clearly, the escape-attempt theory was being carved in stone as the official version of Abe Reles's death.

On November 13, 1941, America learned that the man who'd brought the Mob to its knees was dead. The *New York Times* headline leapt off the front page:

ABE RELES KILLED TRYING TO ESCAPE
Sheet Rope Fails After He Lowers Himself From 6th to 5th Floor of Hotel
MOTIVE PUZZLES POLICE
Informer Against Murder Ring Lived in Dread of Bullets of Former Confederates

Cloaked in artistic license, the paper concocted an image of Reles clinging to his makeshift rope: "Looking southward, he could see surf break against the jetties. He could hear the dolorous clanging of the buoy as it rocked in the tide." Like most of the press coverage of Reles's death, the article was largely a rehash of the escape-attempt theory. Yet there was also an undercurrent that the official story just didn't add up:

Detectives were puzzled. They could not understand why Reles should have tried to escape. For almost twenty months, from the moment he turned informer and came under protective custody, he had shown fear if his guards ever moved out of earshot. Reles had everything to lose by escape, the detectives reasoned. There was no place he could go without going down before the guns and knives of the men who were in the murder ring and were still free.

Other newspapers were equally bewildered. The *Washington Post*, for instance, found it strange "that Reles should try to escape—for his life was forfeit [*sic*] once he was away from his protectors."

If ordinary Americans were shocked by the news of Reles's sensational death, the remaining squealers in O'Dwyer's custody were shaken to the core. Seymour Magoon, once a ruthless enforcer for the Combination, couldn't hide his terror. "I haven't been able to sleep since it happened," the frazzled brute told reporters. He refused to believe that Reles had gone out the window voluntarily. "There must be something in back of it," he fretted. Magoon and his fellow snitches spent endless hours nervously wondering: *Am I next?* That, of course, was precisely what the Mob wanted.

The official story of Reles's death struck most New Yorkers as a joke, a tall tale that would have insulted their intelligence were it not so farcical. Captain McGowan might as well have asked them to believe that the Brooklyn Bridge was for sale. As author Rich Cohen observed years later: "It was a great game in New York, a public murder mystery, a riddle running through heads in the subway, solved at lunch counters, argued over dinner. The death of Reles was the Rubik's Cube of the time, a puzzle on which everyone hopes to prove his wit." And what about the five cops guarding Reles? Not one of them saw anything? Heard anything? Why, the whole thing was preposterous!

Most NYPD cops suspected that the official story was bogus, but they were so thrilled to be rid of Reles that the exact circumstances of his final departure meant little to them. In fact, some made great sport of the way he died. One cop said that "the only law that got him was the law of gravity," while another wisecracking lawman quipped that Reles was "a canary who sang, but couldn't fly." At the top of the chain of command, Reles's grim end was celebrated as a victory for the good guys. "We were well rid of him," Police Commissioner Lewis J. Valentine said frostily. "Brooklyn didn't shed any tears when they buried Reles. We lifted a toast."

■■■

Valentine's remarks raise an interesting question: Should we consider Reles's death as his just desserts? Did he simply reap what he had sown? It's important to remember that from the moment in March 1940 when he cut his deal with the DA until the day he died, Reles was no longer a gangster. He was a state's witness who arguably had earned the right to be judged by whether or not he delivered the goods for the people of New York. Clearly, he had. Reles won the day for the prosecution at the initial Murder, Inc., trials. The best legal talent the Mob's money could buy tried to impeach him as a witness, but two separate juries had found that he was truthful and believed his testimony. Most important, at the time of his death Reles had the Mob on the run— something Valentine, of all people, should have appreciated.

Now for the other side of the equation: Did the DA keep *his* end of the deal? The answer is a resounding no. O'Dwyer, who was ultimately responsible for the security setup at the Half Moon Hotel, had pledged to keep Reles safe. It was all too obvious how miserably he'd failed.

■■■

On November 13, Police Commissioner Valentine announced that the guards on duty in the squealers' suite when Reles died—Detectives Robbins, Boyle, and Moran, and Patrolmen Tempone and McLaughlin— would face a departmental disciplinary trial for negligence. In the meantime, he demoted the three detectives to beat cops, and yanked the two patrolmen off their special duty at the Half Moon Hotel and put them back on the street.

The same day, Detective Celano of the Homicide Squad filed his first report on the Reles case. Taking his cue from Captain McGowan's inexplicable indifference, Celano never returned to the Half Moon to conduct interviews or examine evidence; he simply repeated in his report what he'd seen the previous day. Hewing to the official story, Celano wrote that "an examination of the pipe leading to the radiator valve disclosed a small area which appeared to have been rubbed by something attached to it. It is assumed that the wire which was found attached to the bedsheets had been tied to this and had become loose due to the weight of the subject's body."

At noon, the medical examiner's office handed over the body of Abe Reles to the Misikoff Brothers Jewish Memorial Chapel at 1406 Pitkin Avenue in Brooklyn. In keeping with Orthodox religious practice, the remains were washed, wrapped in a shroud, and placed inside a plain pine box. Shortly after 2:30 p.m., two hired cars arrived at the Reles home at 9102 Avenue A and took the eight mourners—all from the widow's side of the family—to the chapel. (Three police officers accompanied the cortege to provide security.) "The wails of the widow and her mother continued in a minor key until 3 o'clock," the *Brooklyn Eagle* reported. When the gathering filed out for the trip to Mount Carmel Cemetery, photographers tried to get a shot of Mrs. Reles, but she covered her head with the fur collar of her coat and ducked inside one of the cars.

The funeral turned into a spectacle. The widow Reles's wailing continued unabated; her mother and an aunt "supported her as she stumbled, head buried in her hands, through the gravestones to the freshly-dug plot." The attention of the photographers was evidently too much for the widow's father. Cursing, with his fist cocked, he attempted to attack one of the lensmen; the police at the scene were able to restrain him. As the coffin was lowered into the grave, "Mrs. Reles's steady wail was suddenly joined by another, louder one from her mother. The other women, two of them holding up the sagging, plump body of Mrs. Reles, wept copiously." The ceremony, devoid of any religious content, was over in a few minutes.

On the way back to her waiting car, Mrs. Reles shrieked at the photographers: "Damn the newspapers!" Her father, who'd settled down since his earlier outburst, spoke briefly to the press. "We've lived a life of terror for months," he said, referring to his family's fear that the Mob might harm them in its determination to get to Abe Reles. When asked about the death of his notorious son-in-law, he said wearily: "It's better this way."

■■■

As Reles's body was being lowered into the earth, his death was beginning its rise as a hot-button political issue. A bit of background to set the stage: On November 4, the week before Reles's fatal plunge, New Yorkers had gone to the polls to elect a new mayor. The Republican incumbent, Fiorello La Guardia, was seeking an unprecedented third term. The Democrats, eager to retire La Guardia, tapped William

O'Dwyer, who was now a household name because of Murder, Inc. O'Dwyer, who coveted the mayoralty, didn't need to have his arm twisted. "I felt reasonably assured that the massive amount of publicity associated with my work made me a viable candidate," he recalled. "Another advantage I had was that a prosecutor appears constantly to be a fighter against crime and lawlessness and a champion and protector of public order and safety—in short, a desirable candidate for higher office."

The much-anticipated campaign proved to be rather uninspiring. La Guardia spent a good deal of time lobbing insults at O'Dwyer. (While politicking near a produce stand, he lifted up a head of cabbage and cracked: "Reminds me of my opponent's head.") O'Dwyer, for his part, spoke virtually the same bloodless words at every campaign stop: "The mayor has said on numerous occasions that he drove racketeering out of the city. If he did, it's news to me." The results of the November 4 election, however, were stunning: La Guardia won, but by a mere thirteen thousand votes—the closest contest for mayor of New York City since 1904. Shaken by O'Dwyer's strong showing, La Guardia realized that the Brooklyn DA was a long-term political threat whose popularity had to be quashed.

Reles's death was a gift from heaven for La Guardia. What better way to give O'Dwyer a black eye than to harp on the loss of his champion squealer? La Guardia wasted no time in firing his first salvo. Within days of his narrow win at the polls, he told reporters that O'Dwyer hadn't given enough thought to guarding Reles. "I wish there was some other way to take care of star witnesses so that the police would not have to live with them and baby them," he said. "I don't like it." O'Dwyer testily defended the squealers' suite as "a place where [Reles] would not come into contact with other underworld characters, as [he] would have in jail." Score one for La Guardia, who'd succeeded in rattling the DA's cage. In a few weeks, the mayor would attack again—but with more than just words.

■■■

Self-appointed moralists were quick to comment on Reles's death. Syndicated columnist Walter Kiernan wrote a piece titled "Hey Kids! Reles

Was No Hero; Just a Blubberer With a Gun," which appeared in the *Brooklyn Eagle* on November 13. Kiernan was repulsed by the notion of boys looking up to Reles as a role model. "Abe Reles was as strong as the gun in his pocket could make him," Kiernan wrote. "Your big brother could break him apart with his hands but that gun would make the difference. And Reles was of the breed to use it—without warning, without giving the other guy a chance. He would plug your big brother in the back—and you too—if you stood in his way. Get the idea out of your little noodle that any gangster is a hero," he admonished. Trying to dissuade youngsters from lives of crime was a noble cause, but Kiernan was probably sounding an alarm unnecessarily. Most boys of that bygone era idolized baseball players far more than gun-toting thugs.

On November 14, the *New York Times* editorialized about Reles's death. Did the paper use this forum to expose the many flaws in the official story? Not even close. Instead, the *Times* expressed outrage that Reles had been living in the lap of luxury at the Half Moon Hotel. "You find yourself comparing the standard of living enjoyed by the late Abe Reles with the way some other people live under protective custody," the paper fumed. The editorial then contrasted the "fine Boardwalk hotel" where Reles had resided to the "accommodations provided by Hitler" for concentration camp inmates. The comparison was ridiculous and undignified.

As the press and the public buzzed about Reles's demise, District Attorney O'Dwyer continued his curious public silence about Reles's death. Indeed, his first official comments didn't come until November 26, when four of the guards on duty in the squealers' suite when Reles died faced a police department disciplinary trial for neglect of duty. (The fifth guard, Victor Robbins, was ill and had to be tried the following month.) The official charge was that the men "did at some time prior to 7:05 a.m. on November 12, fail and neglect to prevent, discover, or to take action on the escape from custody of one prisoner, viz: Abe Reles, who escaped from the window of Room 623, fell to the roof below, and was killed." The defendants, who were all represented by private counsel, pled not guilty. Captain Bals and Sergeant Divver, their supervisors, were not charged.

Incredibly, O'Dwyer testified voluntarily for the *defense*, despite the fact that the guards were to blame, directly or indirectly, for the death of his star witness and the collapse of the Murder, Inc., probe. "I have the highest opinion of the service that these men rendered," he said under oath. How could he have made such a statement? Most likely, he wanted to polish up the guards' image, help them win an acquittal, and make this the final chapter in the saga of Reles's death. Indeed, O'Dwyer proceeded to put his own spin on the case. It went like this: The Mob was so desperate to kill Reles that an attack on the squealers' suite itself was possible. Since such an attack never took place, the guards must have been doing their jobs. That was O'Dwyer's logic—fuzzy, to say the least. Eagerly, O'Dwyer gave another reason for the judge to go easy on the guards: Since there was never the slightest hint that Reles wanted to flee—he was "afraid to leave the shadow of a policeman," as O'Dwyer himself put it—the guards had no reason to be on the alert for an escape attempt.

Inspector James McGrath, who presented the police department's case against the guards, also turned out to be a boon for the defense. Not only did he decline to cross-examine O'Dwyer, but McGrath accepted the guards' version of the events leading up to Reles's death. He referred to a time gap between 6:45 a.m. and 7:05 a.m. when, by mere chance, no one was checking on Reles; "it must have been during that time," he declared, that Reles tried to escape. McGrath also promoted the lie that former detective Robbins had discovered Reles missing "while on his usual rounds."

Captain Bals and Sergeant Divver, both witnesses for the prosecution, helped the defense even further. The captain continued to rehabilitate the image of the guards by testifying that the Half Moon Hotel detail was "a rather trying assignment," because of the base character of the squealers. When asked how well the guards had carried out this arduous assignment, he responded: "I would say that they carried out their duties to the satisfaction of both myself and O'Dwyer." Divver repeated O'Dwyer's claim that the guards were "instructed to pay particular attention to harm coming to these witnesses from the outside." Like Bals, he had nothing but praise for the men.

Defense counsel could hardly believe things were going so well. Not surprisingly, he asked the judge to throw out the charges against his clients, citing O'Dwyer's testimony that they "were assigned to prevent harm coming to these prisoners [*sic*] from the outside, not specifically to guard them from escape because to escape police custody meant their death on the outside." But the judge decided not to rule on the motion until the defendants themselves had a chance to testify.

James Boyle, the first guard to take the stand, clearly took his cue from the prior witnesses. He said that his primary mission was "to prevent any harm coming to the [squealers] from persons desirous of getting at them from the outside." He noted that Reles was a "willing" detainee; indeed, he cowered in fear behind a guard whenever the doorbell to the suite rang. As for the overnight bed checks of the squealers' rooms, Boyle swore that "all five of us were wide awake, on our toes. Nobody neglected anything. [We] always kept a constant patrol, maintaining supervision day and night." After the other defendants gave virtually identical testimony, both sides rested.

While the trial had its share of the bizarre, in the end the rule of law somehow prevailed. Ignoring O'Dwyer's spin and the other courtroom ploys, the judge decided that the guards had indeed failed to prevent Reles's death. He fined each of them three days' pay, and made permanent the police commissioner's demotion of Detectives Boyle and Moran. (Victor Robbins received the same punishment at his trial in December.)

O'Dwyer must have been deeply discouraged when he was told about the guilty verdicts. His best efforts to clear the squealers' suite guards had failed. Obviously, the Reles case wasn't going away anytime soon.

■■■

On November 30, 1941, Lepke Buchalter, Mendy Weiss, and Louis Capone were convicted of the murder of Joseph Rosen; all three were sentenced to death. Reles was to have appeared at this trial, but it was Allie Tannenbaum's testimony that sealed the fate of the trio. Tannenbaum was in Lepke's office when Lepke ordered the hit, and again when Weiss reported back that the job was done. Following years of appeals, the three were electrocuted at Sing Sing on March 4, 1944. To this day, Lepke remains the only Mob boss ever to be executed by court order in the United States.

■■■

A few days after the Lepke verdict, Captain Bals got an unwelcome surprise. It was a letter from John J. Ryan, assistant chief inspector of the NYPD. Ryan ordered Bals to submit a detailed report on the activities of his Special Investigations Squad: "This report will show the number of hours spent by each man, each day, during the year since April 1, 1941; the nature of the work (giving every detail), and the evidence obtained. The report should also indicate in detail traveling outside of New York as well as within the city, and the reason for time spent in each assignment. Also indicate disbursements and totals for each man." Significantly—given the recent debacle at the Half Moon Hotel—Bals was also ordered to report any situation "where police officers have lived with witnesses and the necessity for it."

Bals was furious. He was sure that Mayor La Guardia was behind Ryan's order, and that the mayor was trying to find something— anything—with which to tarnish O'Dwyer's image. The captain showed the letter to the DA, who was incensed. "Frank, you tell them they can't have this information," O'Dwyer said. "And I don't care who wants the records." Together they located the material and placed it under lock and key. Bals appreciated the DA's support, but he worried that the political strife would only get worse. So after leaving O'Dwyer's office, he went straight to NYPD headquarters, picked up the sheaf of forms required for retirement, then spent the night filling them out. The next day, O'Dwyer tried to talk Bals out of retiring, but he failed. By the end of December, the captain was gone from the force. But the DA didn't let his old crony stay unemployed for long: One month later, he hired Bals as his chief investigator.

On December 31, Detective Celano finally received the results of Reles's toxicology tests. No poisons or drugs were found, but there was a small amount of alcohol (equivalent to a shot of whiskey) in his stomach. Since the liquor hadn't yet been absorbed by the brain, it meant that Reles wasn't drunk when he died. What it *did* mean was that Reles drank this bit of booze very shortly before he died. Supporters of the escape-attempt theory suggested that this was Reles's way of fortifying himself before attempting to escape. But that was out of character for Reles. He never needed liquid courage to carry out his other high-risk endeavors—like committing brutal murders. If the drink was a social one, then who was he socializing with just a short time before plunging to his death? In any event, where had the bottle gone from which the drink was poured? The Homicide Squad didn't find one at the scene, nor did one appear in the crime scene photo of Reles's room.

Detective Celano, however, was not concerned, bothered, or even intrigued by any of this. After all, his boss, Captain McGowan, wanted to close doors, not open them, as far as this case was concerned. So Celano rolled a blank report form into his typewriter and pecked in the test results without comment. Then, with McGowan's blessing, he added an emphatic "CASE CLOSED" to the report.

Less than three weeks after Abe Reles left the Half Moon Hotel in a morgue wagon, the Japanese attacked Pearl Harbor. The riddles swirling around Reles's death were no longer front-page news. But the case refused to die. "Even as America fought the Second World War, Reles continued to intrigue New Yorkers," writer Rich Cohen observed. "There was always some fresh piece of news, some fact, some theory. He continued turning up in newspapers, beaming out from old photographs, refusing to stay dead."

After the war, the controversy would resurface in a major way. And the resulting scandal would forever blacken the reputation of William O'Dwyer—the very man who'd made Abe Reles a household name.

O'Dwyer, however, didn't deserve much sympathy. He brought his promising political future crashing down around him through a combination of arrogance and apathy. The seeds had been sown back in 1940 when, as Brooklyn DA, O'Dwyer made a habit of publicly reviling Albert Anastasia as "the boss murderer" of the Mob. With each incident of name calling, he raised the public's expectation that he would *do* something to bring down the Lord High Executioner, as Anastasia was sometimes referred to in the press. But the DA was just blowing smoke: He didn't actually have a prosecutable case against Anastasia. Then along came Abe Reles. He let the DA in on a dirty little secret: Anastasia was up to his neck in the 1939 rubout of Morris Diamond, the Teamster official whom Lepke suspected of being a rat.

According to Reles, Anastasia chose the site for the Diamond murder, handpicked the hit man, and was at the scene when the victim got clipped. It looked like O'Dwyer had struck gold: Since Reles hadn't participated in the crime itself—he'd simply overheard a planning session for the hit at Anastasia's home—he could provide the testimony of a non-accomplice as required by law. (Angelo Catalano, who drove the getaway car in the Diamond murder, could supply the accomplice testimony.) At long last, the DA had what he needed to hang a murder one rap around Anastasia's neck! Never one to shy away from publicity, O'Dwyer gloated to reporters about having the "perfect murder case" against Anastasia. The day would come when he would rue ever having uttered those words.

After Reles's death, a dire question loomed over the DA's office: Could the case against Anastasia for the Diamond murder proceed without Reles? For some strange reason, O'Dwyer didn't seem to be in any great hurry to find out. He sat on his hands until March 1942—some *four months* after Reles's death—before asking Burton Turkus to prepare a report on whether Anastasia might still be prosecuted successfully. Turkus's report was grim: "The corroboration supplied by Reles expired with Reles," he wrote. "As the investigation now stands, no successful prosecution of Anastasia may be had." Despite this gloomy assessment, Turkus beseeched O'Dwyer not to give up: "Should Anastasia frustrate justice it would be a calamity to society. Somewhere, somehow, corroborative evidence must be available. Investigation focused upon the matter of corroborative evidence should proceed with redoubled effort and every lead should be followed through exhaustively."

Turkus's impassioned plea should have fired up the DA. Instead, O'Dwyer decided to drop his pursuit of Anastasia altogether. He turned to James J. Moran, chief clerk of the DA's office and one of his oldest confidants. Moran, who was "as close to O'Dwyer as his shirt," as one observer said, made arrangements to have the Police Investigation Bureau's wanted cards on Anastasia, Jack Parisi (the hit man who killed Morris Diamond), and Tony Romeo (another one of Anastasia's enforcers) removed from the department's files. These cards were an advisory that the individuals named should be picked up on sight; removal of the cards signified that O'Dwyer was no longer seeking their arrest. On May 4, 1942, slightly more than three weeks after the DA received Turkus's report urging a renewed effort against Anastasia, the three cards were quietly taken out of the bureau's active files. Who actually removed them? It was a familiar face from the past: Sergeant Elwood Divver—Captain Bals's deputy.

Why did O'Dwyer scuttle his "perfect murder case" against Anastasia? For a DA who pined for higher office, the publicity value alone of sending Anastasia to the chair would have been worth the trouble of putting him on trial. Though the answer is still a mystery, one thing is certain: O'Dwyer kept his about-face a secret, deceiving the public into believing that he was still doggedly pursuing "the boss murderer."

Soon after their wanted cards were lifted, Anastasia, Parisi, and Romeo—all of whom had gone into hiding when Reles began squealing—magically reappeared in Brooklyn. Their Mob buddies greeted them like returning war heroes. Anastasia's liberty, however, was short-lived: In mid-1942 he was drafted into the army. But tough-guy Anastasia didn't volunteer for combat. He finagled an assignment training troops in the fine art of longshoring at Fort Indiantown Gap, Pennsylvania. In late 1945, he was mustered out of the army and made a triumphant return to his waterfront empire. Tony Romeo's newfound freedom was brief. In June 1942, his corpse was found floating in a creek in Wilmington, Delaware. He had been savagely beaten, then used for target practice. Rumor had it that Anastasia ordered the hit because he doubted Romeo's loyalty.

As for O'Dwyer, he took a leave of absence from the DA's office on June 1, 1942, to join the army. He spent most of the war years investigating fraudulent practices in the procurement of military supplies. In 1944, President Roosevelt appointed him as chief of the Economic Section of the Allied Commission; O'Dwyer was sent to Italy as the president's personal envoy to the Foreign Economic Administration. (He was also awarded the rank of brigadier general, though the title was largely ceremonial.) When he returned to New York City in 1945, O'Dwyer resigned as DA to pursue a second bid for mayor. He was confident of victory: After three consecutive terms, his old nemesis, Fiorello La Guardia, had decided not to run. Once again, O'Dwyer adopted his crime-buster persona for the campaign. "If [gangsters] are here they had better pack up and get out fast, because when I go in as mayor it will be just as hot for them in 1946 as it was in Brooklyn in 1940," he crowed to supporters. "They will travel the same trail that led others to the electric chair."

The Republicans had no intention of giving up without a fight. They hatched a devious plan to sink O'Dwyer's candidacy. It went like this: Thomas E. Dewey, who'd parlayed his reputation as a relentless racket buster into the governorship of New York in 1942 and 1946, appointed fellow Republican George J. Beldock Jr., an attorney, to fill the remainder of O'Dwyer's term as DA. Beldock immediately launched a grand jury investigation into O'Dwyer's effectiveness in office. The panel swiftly issued a report skewering the former DA for coddling Anastasia:

1. We find that every case against Albert Anastasia was abandoned, neglected, or pigeon-holed.
2. We find that William O'Dwyer, as district attorney, neglected to complete a single prosecution against Anastasia.
3. We find that there admittedly was available competent legal evidence, sufficient to warrant the indictment, conviction, and punishment of Anastasia for murder in a case described by William O'Dwyer himself as "a perfect murder case."

The report continued to slash away at O'Dwyer: "The complete failure to prosecute the 'overlord' of organized crime in Brooklyn, where the evidence was sufficient to warrant his conviction, is so revolting that we cannot permit these disclosures to be filed away in the same manner that the evidence against Anastasia was put 'in the files.'" In a final swipe, O'Dwyer was excoriated for his "negligence, incompetence, and flagrant irresponsibility." Beldock released the report just days before the November 6 election in order to cause maximum damage to O'Dwyer's campaign and unnerve the candidate himself.

O'Dwyer, who was caught off-guard by the speedy release of the report, seemed genuinely concerned that the publicity over his failure to prosecute Anastasia for the Diamond murder might cost him the election. On the evening of October 30, 1945, he went on live radio to give an urgent response to the grand jury's claims. "As long as Abe Reles was alive we had a perfectly good case against Albert Anastasia," he said. "But the day Reles went through the window and was killed, that particular case, for want of corroboration, was no longer a clear case." O'Dwyer was confident that this explanation would put an end to the controversy.

Actually, he'd stepped right into a trap. On live radio the next evening, Beldock sarcastically demolished O'Dwyer's explanation:

> Well, Mr. O'Dwyer, you knew you had a perfectly good case against Albert Anastasia in March or April of 1940. Your trial prosecutor used the testimony of Abe Reles to send four killers to the electric chair. As long as Reles was good and lively [*sic*] and talking his head off, why, Mr. O'Dwyer, did you fail to send him before a Brooklyn grand jury against Anastasia? What was there about Anastasia? You let Reles talk about everybody else. Why was he muzzled when it came to Anastasia?

The logic of Beldock's argument was irrefutable: Why indeed had O'Dwyer waited until it was too late? Chastened, O'Dwyer decided on a new tack: avoid the issue altogether. He ceased all mention of Anastasia and the "perfect murder case" in his speeches. Instead, he reminded voters of his wartime service, and of the good old days when he'd sent seven gangsters to the electric chair. The strategy of avoidance worked: On election day, November 6, 1945, O'Dwyer defeated his lackluster opponent, Republican judge Jonah J. Goldstein, by a comfortable margin. Sadly, he'd also evaded responsibility for having allowed Anastasia to get away with murder.

A couple of interesting footnotes to O'Dwyer's term as mayor. Shortly after he was sworn in, two of his cronies were back in the news. First, James J. Moran, the man behind the removal of the three wanted cards from the NYPD's files, had the scathing Beldock grand jury report about O'Dwyer expunged from the record on a legal technicality (the report quoted grand jury testimony, which is supposed to be secret). Second, O'Dwyer promoted Frank Bals, the architect of the failed security arrangements at the Half Moon Hotel, to the plum job of seventh deputy police commissioner. Though Bals stayed on the job for only a few months, the new post gave him the luxury of retiring with a pension worth more than double that of his previous rank of captain.

■ ■ ■

O'Dwyer was reelected mayor in 1949, but grave trouble was on the horizon. Late that year, Brooklyn DA Miles McDonald began looking into claims that bookies were bribing cops and city officials to the tune of millions of dollars a year. (The probe was prompted by a series of exposés in the *Brooklyn Eagle*.) One Mob bookie claimed to have given twenty thousand dollars to James J. Moran as a "contribution" to O'Dwyer's campaign fund. As the probe picked up steam, O'Dwyer seemed to come undone. He denounced McDonald's inquiry as, among other things, "a witch hunt, and a war of nerves made popular by Hitler." New Yorkers were stunned by the ferocity of the mayor's remarks. Many wondered if he had something to hide.

O'Dwyer's harangue caused Ed Flynn, a member of the Democratic National Committee from the Bronx—and one of the party's power brokers—to wonder about the same thing. It was clear to him that O'Dwyer was now a liability to the party; somehow the mayor had to be put beyond the reach of investigators. Using his considerable political clout, Flynn arranged a meeting with President Harry Truman to discuss damage control. Truman agreed that something had to be done about O'Dwyer.

On August 14, 1950, the White House made a startling announcement: President Truman had nominated O'Dwyer to be ambassador to Mexico! The president cited O'Dwyer's command of the Spanish language and his friendship with Mexican president Miguel Alemán as the reasons for the nomination. The Senate, unaware that the nomination was motivated by political expediency, quickly confirmed him. True to form, O'Dwyer used what was left of his fading political influence to appoint his loyal buddy, the ubiquitous James J. Moran, to a lucrative, lifetime job as commissioner of the city's Board of Water Supply. (Moran didn't get to enjoy O'Dwyer's largesse for long: In the coming years, he would spend close to a decade behind bars on various extortion and perjury convictions.)

Shortly after O'Dwyer had settled into a comfortable routine in Mexico City, trouble found him once again. In March 1951, the Senate Crime Committee (better known as the Kefauver Committee after its chairman, Democrat Estes Kefauver of Tennessee) announced plans to hold public hearings later that month in New York City as part of its national probe of organized crime. The five-man committee had drawn up a long list of potential witnesses; William O'Dwyer and Frank Bals were near the top.

Although it is not generally known, O'Dwyer had been in secret contact with the committee while he was still mayor. Convinced that Kefauver and his colleagues were planning to poke around in some potentially embarrassing areas—Reles's death and the Diamond murder case to name just two—O'Dwyer tried to ingratiate himself with the committee early on. Acting the part of the elder statesman of crime fighting, he traveled to Washington to discuss the scourge of the Mob with Senator Kefauver and Rudolf Halley, the committee's chief counsel. The dialogue continued after O'Dwyer returned to New York City. "Halley came to see me at City Hall on several occasions," O'Dwyer recalled, "and both he and Kefauver thanked me for helping them get started."

But all of this goodwill turned sour. Soon after O'Dwyer began his tenure as ambassador, Halley asked Brooklyn DA Miles McDonald for a copy of the scathing Beldock Grand Jury report from 1945. Halley wasn't pleased by what he read: It was clear that O'Dwyer had tried to sell him a bill of goods about how professionally the Reles and Diamond matters had been handled when he was DA. By the time O'Dwyer was formally invited to New York City to testify, Halley and several committee members were itching for a fight.

It would be a very public confrontation. The committee's hearings were carried on live television, and each day more than twenty million Americans sat mesmerized by the stark, black-and-white images of menacing gangsters and fidgety politicians testifying under the glaring klieg lights. As Kefauver remembered: "Businesses were paralyzed; many movie halls became ghost halls—some even installed a television and invited the public to come in free and watch; housewives did their ironing and mending in front of their sets."

Mindful of the huge television audience, Kefauver and his colleagues didn't want to botch the questioning of O'Dwyer. So on March 15, 1951, they sharpened their knives on his buddy Frank Bals. (By this time, Bals had resigned from the police force for the second time and was living in comfortable retirement in Florida.)

Senator Charles Tobey, an ornery, Bible-thumping, seventy-one-year-old Republican from New Hampshire, was the committee's attack dog. He treated Bals like a child, and Bals responded by putting his foot in his mouth at almost every opportunity. Sporting a pair of green eyeshades, Tobey asked Bals for his theory about Reles's death. In all seriousness, Bals suggested that Reles had been trying to play a prank on his guards. The packed hearing room exploded in laughter and hisses; Kefauver pounded his gavel until order was restored. Seemingly oblivious to the uproar, Bals continued. Reles, he explained, intended to lower himself to the room below, climb back up the stairs to the sixth floor, knock on the door of the squealers' suite, then delight in the astonished look on the guards' faces. When Tobey ridiculed this scenario as "the peek-a-boo theory," it brought down the house.

Kefauver again gaveled the crowd to order. Tobey began mercilessly needling Bals about why the guards hadn't prevented Reles's demise: "So Reles is found dead five or six floors below, with policemen on guard to see that it didn't happen, and I asked you in the confidential hearing we held how you explained it, and you said—this is a wonderful answer—you said 'I imagine they all fell asleep at the same time.'" Once again, the chairman was forced to restore order to the proceedings. Having made mincemeat of Bals, Tobey fired one last salvo: "The whole thing [Reles's death], from the standpoint of the citizen and the country, as well as New York, is a tawdry mess, smells under heaven, and I don't believe that the honest truth has been told about it; probably won't be until the day of judgment."

The committee was now ready for O'Dwyer. The former mayor was in a foul mood from the moment his plane landed in the city he once governed: "The day I left for Mexico to serve as ambassador, New York City put on a parade and ceremonies for me. Crowds lined the streets downtown. Now, when I returned to testify, few people showed up at the airport outside of my family."

He was still sullen when he entered the hearing room on March 19: "There was noise and confusion everywhere," he later complained. "The television lights were glaring and hot, and I was suffering from a high temperature, a combination designed to make me most uncomfortable. Wiping the perspiration off of my face was to be avoided, lest it give the impression that it was the subject matter rather than the heat causing the discomfort." Oddly, the press saw a completely different person; one reporter described O'Dwyer as being "in excellent physical condition, with a face well tanned by the Mexican sun."

If O'Dwyer thought that the disappointing reception at the airport would be the low point of his visit, he was sadly mistaken. The first sign of trouble came during his opening remarks before the committee. After he had droned on for almost an hour about his achievements as mayor, Kefauver finally interrupted: "I am afraid your voice may give out. It might be well to get on with our inquiry." O'Dwyer, clearly miffed, acquiesced. Chief Counsel Rudolf Halley began firing questions at the witness about why Anastasia was never even indicted for the murder of Morris Diamond. Dazed by the harsh treatment he thought he was receiving—he later accused the committee of "ambushing" him—O'Dwyer did little but offer his same tired excuse that the case "went out the window" when Reles died. When Halley countered that Reles had been prepared to testify for a considerable amount of time before his death—*twenty months* to be exact—O'Dwyer blurted out that he, O'Dwyer, had been too busy with other murder cases. Murmurs of disbelief swept through the audience.

When that excuse fell on deaf ears, O'Dwyer tried the blame game. He asserted that Thomas Craddock Hughes, who had been acting DA while O'Dwyer was in the army, should have gone after Anastasia. It was all Hughes's fault. Halley must have been anticipating that answer, because he produced a *New York Times* article from 1943 in which O'Dwyer was quoted as saying he was "greatly pleased" with the job Hughes was doing. Red-faced, O'Dwyer said he had no recollection of the article or the quote.

Senator Tobey, who'd been champing at the bit, finally pounced:

Q: What is your version of the death of Reles?

O'DWYER: That he tried to escape.

Q: Then your testimony contravenes the testimony of Mr. Bals, whose thesis is that he didn't try to escape, that he rigged the sheet and the wire and let himself out of the window with the intention of climbing in the floor below and coming up and tapping on the door and saying, "Peek-a-boo, I'm back again." You knew that, didn't you?

O'DWYER: I couldn't tell what was in Reles's mind. All I know was that there was the rope [*sic*] and there was the sheet, and there was the window underneath which he could reach, and it slipped, and he fell and was killed; what he was trying to do will never be known.

Q: You know Bals, don't you?

O'DWYER: Yes, sir.

Q: And you appointed him, didn't you?

O'DWYER: I did, indeed.

Q: Wasn't he a flat tire?

O'Dwyer was stung by the accusation—albeit couched in good old boy slang—that Bals was a dimwit. His eyes welling with tears, O'Dwyer tried to defend his friend by praising his bravery, but Tobey would have none of it: "If you are trying to build up a case for Bals before this committee," he snarled, "you will have a very hard time doing it. Bals made a spectacle of himself, and he gave the flimsiest excuse possible about the death of Reles."

The rancor between Tobey and O'Dwyer over Reles's death only got worse. At one point, Tobey said flat-out that he believed Reles's guards threw him out the window. O'Dwyer was incensed. "Do you *know* they did that, Senator?" he asked. "That is my theory," Tobey replied. "Have you any facts upon which to base it, sir?" O'Dwyer inquired. "Only intuition and horse sense," the senator retorted. "I will not answer a question based on intuition and horse sense," O'Dwyer snapped.

Counsel Halley jumped into the fray. "At least there is some basis in fact for Senator Tobey's theory. There are those who have seen the pictures [of Reles's corpse] and feel that a man going out of the window on his own power, unless he took a running jump, could not have gotten that far from the building, isn't that so?" O'Dwyer had no fight left in him. "Have it that way," he responded wearily.

O'Dwyer's ordeal lasted for two days. When it finally ended, he was a broken man. His once imposing figure—immaculately dressed, impeccably groomed—was a distant memory. He appeared haggard and disheveled, with thin strands of silver hair stuck to the side of his head. The public had turned its back on him, too: Opinion polls showed that most Americans thought his testimony had been an unmitigated disaster. The White House was inundated with demands that he be replaced as ambassador. His reputation in tatters, his dreams of high political office shattered beyond repair, O'Dwyer couldn't get back to Mexico fast enough.

Given the thrashing that Kefauver and company dealt O'Dwyer, it's no surprise that the committee's final report slammed him for his cavalier attitude toward Reles's death:

> Asked what he did to establish responsibility for the loss of his most important witness against [Anastasia], O'Dwyer explained that he and the police commissioner considered it a pure case of negligence on the part of the police officers. O'Dwyer conceded he had appeared as a voluntary witness on behalf of the men at the [departmental] trial, stating that they were blameless. He insisted that Bals, who was in charge of the detail, could not be held responsible for something which happened in the dead of night, when he was not there, even though he was the one who assigned the men to their task and supervised the arrangements.

Then came the knockout punch:

> Neither O'Dwyer nor his appointees took any effective action against the top echelons of the gambling, narcotics, waterfront,

murder, or bookmaking rackets. In fact, his actions impeded promising investigations of such rackets. His failure to follow up concrete evidence of organized crime, particularly in the case of Murder, Inc., *contributed to the growth of racketeering and gangsterism in New York City.*

If this judgment of O'Dwyer seems overly harsh—after all, he wasn't a comic-book superhero who could eradicate the Mob single-handedly—his response to the charges seems overly histrionic: "You don't kill public men today," he told a reporter after the Kefauver Committee's report was released. "You smear them to death."

O'Dwyer resigned as ambassador in December 1952, but he chose to remain in Mexico to pursue business interests. The following year, a popular American magazine published an article about his spectacular fall from grace. The title of the piece perfectly captured the humiliation of O'Dwyer's exile. It was called "The Man Who Won't Come Home."

PART III

SLEUTHING

More than twenty million American viewers watched Frank Bals and William O'Dwyer self-destruct on live television. Back in Brooklyn, the DA's office was flooded with phone calls, letters, and telegrams ridiculing Bals and O'Dwyer, and demanding that Reles's death be reinvestigated. Actually, DA Miles McDonald had already decided to reopen the case; in fact, he had confidentially notified the Kefauver Committee of his intentions after O'Dwyer's first disastrous day on the stand. The news was supposed to be kept secret until a formal announcement could be made, but Senator Tobey couldn't resist rubbing it in O'Dwyer's face during one of their heated exchanges: "I am thankful that District Attorney McDonald's office is going to make a further investigation into this," Tobey growled. According to a *New York Times* reporter, O'Dwyer seemed to blanch at the revelation.

McDonald didn't make his decision lightly. Even after ten years, Reles's death was still a touchy subject to many in the DA's office and the NYPD. With reputations to preserve and careers to protect, they considered the case closed and wanted to keep it that way. McDonald was far more concerned, however, with the potential life-and-death consequences of reopening the case. He was all too aware that if the Mob had killed Reles (as many suspected), it might try to thwart a new inquiry by whacking anyone called to testify. The last thing the DA wanted to do was incite a bloody purge like the one Lepke had unleashed back in 1937, when the Mob boss ordered the murder of at least a dozen former associates to silence them.

Who could McDonald entrust with the sensitive, daunting task of reopening the Reles case? He decided not to ask the governor for a special prosecutor because that would have meant giving up control of the probe—not an option for such a politically sensitive and, in some quarters, unwelcome inquiry. Fortunately, he had to look no further than his own office to find a suitable choice.

Edward Silver, fifty-three, was McDonald's chief assistant. After graduating from the Harvard Law School in 1924, Silver established his own firm in New York City the following year. Following four years in private practice, he began a career in public service. Silver's first post was the US Attorney's office, where he served with distinction until 1945. In 1946, he accepted Miles McDonald's offer to become chief assistant district attorney for Kings County (Brooklyn). A quiet, unassuming man, he was respected for his thoroughness in the courtroom—and for the long hours he put in.

Silver was given a good deal of freedom to direct the investigation, though he had to make do with a relatively small staff: two assistant DAs and a few NYPD detectives. Their legwork, especially in tracking down and interviewing the scores of witnesses who were ignored in 1941, would prove to be invaluable.

Silver's inquiry would follow the traditional course of a grand jury probe. After gathering testimony and physical evidence, he would review the material, then present witnesses and exhibits to a grand jury. If, after hearing Silver's case, the jurors believed Reles's death was a homicide—and the perpetrator(s) could be identified—they would hand down indictments for murder, manslaughter, or a similar charge. If the suspected killer or killers were dead, if Reles died by accident or by his own hand, or if they could not reach a firm conclusion about the case, they would instead issue a report (also known as a presentment) about what they believed was the reason for Reles's untimely end.

■■■

After familiarizing himself with the facts of the case, Silver decided that his first order of business would be to confront a pair of potentially explosive rumors about Reles's death that had been floating around since the Kefauver Committee hearings. One rumor stemmed from some off-the-cuff remarks Senator Tobey made during his grilling of Frank Bals. The senator had suggested that the single crime scene photo of Reles's fully clothed body may have hidden serious, if not fatal, injuries he sustained *before* going out the window. Tobey had even managed to cajole Frank Bals into agreeing with him:

Q: That photograph wouldn't show any stabs in the body, would it?

BALS: It would not.

Q: No, and it wouldn't show any bullet holes, would it?

BALS: It would not.

Silver briefly considered exhuming Reles's body in order to determine if he'd been stabbed or shot before his fall. But Dr. Thomas Gonzales, the chief medical examiner of New York City, told Silver that it would be a waste of time for two reasons: The doctor who performed the original autopsy would not have missed something as obvious as a stab wound or bullet wound; and, since the body was now just a skeleton, there would be no evidence of a wound unless the knife or bullet had struck bone. Silver decided against digging up Reles. Instead, he would try to put the rumor to rest by having Dr. Gonzales interpret the autopsy report under oath.

The other rumor involved a "mystery witness" who allegedly told friends that she'd seen Reles being pushed out of his window back in 1941. An anonymous caller to Ed Silver's office identified the mystery witness as Lessie Gold, a twenty-four-year-old nurse living in New Jersey. When Silver's investigators brought her in for questioning, she told them that during a stroll along the Coney Island Boardwalk in 1941, "I saw a body falling to the sun deck of the Half Moon Hotel. It was a man dressed in dark clothing. Subsequently, I read in the paper that Abe Reles had fallen from one of the windows, and I associated that fact with what I had seen." Gold said that she'd kept her lips sealed for ten years out of fear that the Mob was involved in the incident, and that as an eyewitness her life might be in danger. But she firmly denied telling anybody that the falling man was *definitely* Reles, or that she saw him being *pushed* out of the window.

Three aspects of Gold's story led Silver to conclude that her information was useless. First, Gold recalled that she had been wearing warm-weather clothing at the time of the incident, but Reles died on a cool night in November. Second, she said that the incident took place in the early evening, but Reles was still alive at that time. Third, she claimed that the body fell to the hotel's sundeck, but Reles landed on the kitchen extension roof, which was on a different side of the hotel. Whatever Gold may have witnessed that day on the Boardwalk—if indeed she witnessed anything at all—Silver believed that it couldn't have been Abe Reles's fatal fall.

■■■

New Yorkers were excited by the prospect of a new probe into Reles's death. Several citizens even volunteered to help Silver. One, Anthony Corpolongo, sent him a letter stating that the Mob had killed Reles: "They bagged him because of the mobsters that went to the chair. There was 15 grand payed [*sic*] out for that piece of work." Corpolongo was eager to help catch the killers, but first he needed a favor: Could Silver convince the parole board to free him? Corpolongo, it turned out, was serving time in Clinton Prison in Dannemora, New York, for armed robbery. Silver refused to get involved with the parole board, but he did send an investigator to the prison. Corpolongo said that he learned about Reles's murder five years earlier from a former inmate known as "Blackie." Blackie told him that "Reles was killed because certain people in the Mob was [*sic*] afraid that he would send them to the chair, because at that time he was telling everything to the District Attorney. I asked him how he knew this and he replied 'I know it on good authority.' Blackie would not mention any names to me or give me any further information." Despite an exhaustive effort, the mysterious Blackie was never identified. Silver eventually classified Corpolongo's story as yet another red herring.

Armchair detectives offered their assistance, too. Almost to a man, they urged Silver to focus on Reles's guards. "I wonder whether the officers have gone through the lie detector test," one correspondent mused. "If any officer refuses the lie-detector test it should be possible to effect his dismissal. Or the publicity about his refusal would break him down eventually." Warming to his subject, he continued: "If an attempt was made to pick police who would commit murder, it seems probable that only some of them were trustworthy [*sic*]. The others must be disposed of by giving them a drug in food or drink so that they would sleep during the proceedings."

Someone calling himself "A Loyal Citizen" proposed that Reles's guards be subjected to "the third degree" live on national television. While "Loyal Citizen" never explained what he meant by the third degree, he was certain that it would force the guards to reveal "who ordered them to pitch him [Reles] out." He urged Silver to be fearless in seeking the truth: "The people are behind you absolutely," he wrote reassuringly.

Another anonymous source claimed he knew the dark truth about November 12, 1941. "Now listen to this," his cryptic letter began. "The night Abe Reles was killed this is exactly what happened. They planted a few guys there to get this Abe Reles to climb down the sheets from the bed. Told him he was in a very hot spot and scared him stiff. Told him all the cops was [*sic*] sleeping. When he passed the window below, the other guy cut the line. Corpses tell no tales."

■■■

Of course, not everyone was thrilled at the prospect of revisiting Reles's death. Several members of the Reles family were completely against it. Reles's mother, for one, definitely didn't want the case resurrected. "She appeared to be very much disturbed about the publicity that this matter is receiving," an investigator told Silver, "which she feels brings disgrace to her and her family and she is very desirous of keeping this matter as quiet as possible." Her objections were mild, however, compared with those of Reles's widow, Rose. Rose was so bitterly opposed to reopening the case that, as we shall see, she made it her mission to derail Silver's inquiry.

■■■

Early on in his investigation, the usually tight-lipped Silver was less than cautious in his dealings with the press. He dropped titillating morsels about having uncovered "some new and very interesting information which hitherto has never been revealed in the Reles case." He also made provocative remarks about specific items of evidence. Concerning the bedsheets found near Reles's body, he said: "I don't know whether they were used to climb out on or were used as props."

As the inquiry progressed, however, Silver learned not to be so chatty with the press. That may be why some media figures made a habit of promising their readers or listeners sensational revelations about the case, rather than accept an information blackout. Famed gossip columnist Walter Winchell, the intermediary in Lepke's surrender, was one of the worst offenders. On the June 10, 1951, broadcast of his popular radio show, Winchell made a tantalizing claim: "A sensational break is expected soon in the Reles case. The theory is being switched from accident to murder and a top cop will be accused of the job." Ed Silver tried to contact Winchell about the supposed bombshell before it could be detonated over the airwaves, but his calls were never returned. Not that it mattered: Winchell never produced the sensational break he'd promised his audience.

Regrettably, some members of the print media resorted to tabloid journalism. It was not unusual to find a newspaper article about the case accompanied by a photograph of manufactured evidence. Beneath the arresting headline "DID ABE RELES FALL OR WAS HE PUSHED?" the New York *Daily News* printed a photo, taken "at the time of Reles's death," purporting to show a reporter examining the makeshift rope in Reles's room. This scene, however, had clearly been staged. The configuration of the room proves that it was not Reles's, and the bedsheets are shown tied to a water pipe. The real makeshift rope, of course, was found on the extension roof near Reles's body.

Articles about the reopening of the case turned up in some unexpected places. In the April 25, 1951, issue of *People Today*, a glossy celebrity magazine, the evil Reles was featured alongside national icons like Joe DiMaggio and Charles Lindbergh. The article, "Questions Kefauver Didn't Ask," demanded to know why the committee had failed to interrogate "the policemen guarding Abe Reles when he fell," and "the medical examiner who studied Reles's brain and stomach." A full-page photo of Reles, his menacing eyes glaring at the reader, appeared with the article.

Burton Turkus, the former Murder, Inc., prosecutor, contributed in his own way to the media hype. In an interview with the New York *Daily News*, he scorned Frank Bals's prank theory, arguing that although Reles was a practical joker, "he would never play a joke if there was a threat of bodily harm to him. He loved himself dearly." Turkus also nixed the theory that Reles had been trying to escape, recalling that Reles knew Mob killers would make short work of him in the outside world. Turkus capitalized on the reopening of the case by writing a series of syndicated newspaper articles. He also penned a book, *Murder, Inc.: The Story of the Syndicate,* which was published while Silver's inquiry was still in progress. (The book caught Hollywood's attention; in 1960, it was made into a movie starring actor Peter Falk as Abe Reles.)

■■■

Silver had to contend with some major obstacles right from the start. He discovered early on that not a single piece of physical evidence had been submitted for forensic testing in 1941. As a veteran prosecutor, he found it beyond belief that this elementary step in any death investigation hadn't been taken. But the director of the police lab quickly confirmed it: "Search of the records reveals no field run to the scene, nor the processing of any evidence in reference to the death of said Reles," he wrote in a letter to Silver. To make matters worse, Silver found that some vital pieces of evidence, such as Reles's shoes and clothes, had been discarded by the NYPD.

The Half Moon Hotel itself was also an important piece of physical evidence. Silver had planned to have his investigators take extensive measurements at the site, but here again he ran into a huge setback: The building had been significantly altered since 1941. From 1944 until 1946, it served as a naval hospital where more than five thousand sailors convalesced. The navy reported that "considerable redecoration, alteration, and repairing" went into the conversion. The ballroom was made into a mess hall, the grill into a chapel, and the lounge into a soda fountain. Other changes included construction of surgical rooms, a laboratory, a pharmacy, an X-ray room, a dental office, recreational facilities, and a library. When the navy left in 1946, the building was converted into a retirement home; at one point or another, substantial changes had been made to almost every room.

Another enormous stumbling block was the death of several key witnesses, chief among them medical examiner Dr. Gregory Robillard and Captain John McGowan of the Homicide Squad. Robillard, who passed away in 1949, would have been quizzed about the specifics of Reles's injuries, as well as what prompted him to scribble the cryptic notation "Withhold information by order of D.A." on Reles's autopsy report.

If McGowan, who died in 1948, had been around, Silver would have grilled him about his slipshod handling of the physical evidence—including his failure to submit a single item to the police lab—and his staggering decision not to interview any of the guests, tenants, or employees of the Half Moon Hotel. Silver also had a spate of tough questions that he would have asked McGowan about the escape-attempt theory, such as:

■ Reles was a meticulous planner when it came to committing murder. Wouldn't he have been just as meticulous—even more so—when planning and carrying out his escape? Would he have gambled with his life on a flimsy, hastily made escape device?

■ According to the escape-attempt theory, Reles tried to flee sometime between 6:45 a.m. and 7:15 a.m. on November 12. But weather records for that day show that sunrise was at 6:40 a.m. Would Reles have tried to escape during daylight? Would he have taken the chance on being seen dangling from his makeshift rope by someone taking an early morning stroll along the Boardwalk?

■ When the police searched Reles's body, they found just $2.35 in his pockets. Would he have begun his days on the run, hunted by the Mob and the cops, with such a paltry sum?

■ Reles allegedly tried to break into the room below his own as part of his escape plan. But how could he have known for certain that the room was vacant?

- If Reles had gotten into room 523, could he have gone down the remaining five stories of the hotel, ambled through the lobby, and slipped by the guards at the hotel's entrances, all without being recognized by a single soul? Wouldn't that have been quite a feat for someone whose face regularly graced the papers, and who was well known to many of the hotel's employees and long-term guests?

- If Reles had somehow made it to the street, what then? The escape-attempt theory makes no mention of a getaway car. What if an accomplice had left a car in the hotel's parking lot for Reles to use? Why didn't McGowan take down the license plates of the vehicles in the lot and then match them up with their owners? Or did the captain want the world to believe that Reles would have started his life on the lam by hoofing it?

These questions called out for answers. With McGowan dead, however, there would be nothing but a resounding silence.

■■■

Of the scores of prospective witnesses on Silver's list, William O'Dwyer and Senator Charles Tobey were two of the most eagerly anticipated. But both men balked at testifying at the new inquiry. In a letter to Silver, Tobey said he didn't have any firsthand information about Reles's death:

> Statements made by me at the [Kefauver] hearings were based upon suppositions that were designed to prompt pertinent answers from witnesses . . . But upon questioning Bals, and listening to his ludicrous testimony that all six [*sic*] policemen, who guarded Reles fell asleep at the same time, very serious doubts [were raised] in my mind. [Reles's] being out of the way would be welcomed by many parties because he was the outstanding witness in the Anastasia case and had never testified. So I have no facts or actual evidence to give with reference to

Reles's death other than to review my utterances and expressions at the Kefauver hearings, and express the doubts which I had and still have in the cause of his death and the motives therefore. However, if after you read this you still feel that I should appear, I would be very happy to come.

Silver promptly scratched Tobey's name off the witness list. It was no great loss. The senator was a demagogue who enjoyed playing to the gallery. He obviously had no interest in revisiting the Reles case now that his soapbox on national television was gone.

As for O'Dwyer, it had been taken for granted that he would testify at the new inquiry; headlines like "RELES DEATH JURY TO HEAR O'DWYER" made it seem all but certain. But O'Dwyer was loath to testify. The idea of returning to New York City to face yet another humiliating inquiry was far from appealing. The fact that New York DA Frank Hogan had already expressed an interest in quizzing O'Dwyer about new allegations of corruption made it even less so.

Silver sent a telegram to O'Dwyer in Mexico City inviting him to testify, but the ambassador didn't respond. Peeved, Silver told reporters that he was weighing "a further course of action" to persuade O'Dwyer to appear, and this fueled rumors that a subpoena might be in the offing. Word must have reached O'Dwyer that the situation was turning ugly, because he suddenly responded to Silver's original invitation:

I have received your telegram relative to the death of Reles, ten years ago, which, at the time, was of great public interest and received widespread publicity. The official investigation into the circumstances surrounding Reles' death was in charge of [*sic*] Mayor La Guardia and his Police Commissioner, Louis [*sic*] Valentine. Foul play was not suggested by anyone or from any source concerned with or interested in ascertaining the facts surrounding Reles' death.

I have never had, nor have I now, any knowledge of any fact or circumstance supporting such a theory. In the absence of such information, I fail to see how my appearance could serve any useful purpose. Should you or the Grand Jury send a representative to Mexico, I shall be pleased to see him and answer any questions within my knowledge which may be pertinent to Reles' death.

The response was typical O'Dwyer. In his haste to wash his hands of the case by pointing out that the mayor and the police commissioner were "in charge" of the original investigation, he glossed over the fact that Reles died in the borough where he, O'Dwyer, had been the chief law enforcement officer at the time. His claim that "Foul play was not suggested by anyone or from any source concerned with or interested in ascertaining the facts surrounding Reles' death" was patently ridiculous. For a decade, reasonable people concerned about the case had been suggesting exactly that.

Silver ultimately decided not to have O'Dwyer testify at all. It's not completely clear why, though politics may have played a part. O'Dwyer was extremely well liked in Mexico. In fact, Miguel Alemán, the country's president, condemned O'Dwyer's pummeling by the Kefauver Committee as a "political attack" on "the most popular ambassador we have ever had from the United States," and sent his own private plane to fetch O'Dwyer from New York as a "gesture of affection." (O'Dwyer hopped aboard and returned to Mexico City on a nonstop flight.) Silver may have been concerned that by subpoenaing such a beloved figure, he might anger the Mexican government and set off an international incident. By that measure, O'Dwyer simply wasn't worth the potential trouble.

Did Reles die while trying to flee from the Half Moon Hotel? For Ed Silver, it was the proverbial $64,000 question. The official story had Reles crashing to his death during a botched escape attempt. But that version of events never caught on with the public because it couldn't clear a simple logical hurdle: Why would Reles willingly put himself in the gunsights of the hit men who were salivating at the prospect of blowing him away? Or as he himself put it so succinctly: "Anywhere in the world they'd find me, if I was on the outside. And they'd knock me off!" When the men who were closest to Reles during his nearly two years in protective custody—his guards, Frank Bals, Elwood Divver— were questioned on the morning of his death, they agreed that for all of his tough-guy swagger, Reles's knees went weak at the thought of being at large in the outside world.

Ten years had passed. Silver wondered: Did those same witnesses still feel that Reles's fear of the Mob would have kept him from trying to bolt from the Half Moon Hotel? Elwood Divver (who'd retired from the NYPD in 1948) gave Silver a peek inside Reles's tortured psyche:

Q: From your talks with Reles, would you say that he was in fear of forces that existed outside of his suite?

DIVVER: I would say yes to that.

Q: And by forces outside, I am talking about members of some mob whether they [*sic*] were Anastasia, Lepke or any other group?

DIVVER: Yes.

Q: When you say he was in fear was it a serious fear?

DIVVER: A very deep seated fear.

Q: Try to give us a description of the type of fear or why you say it was a deep seated fear.

DIVVER: I believe he was thoroughly familiar with underworld customs and practices, and knowing that he had given very damaging testimony and information to the District Attorney, he, no doubt, was fully convinced that he didn't have long to live unless under very special precautions.

Q: Do you remember incidents where he actually showed his fear by staying close to people or hugging walls?

DIVVER: On many occasions.

Q: Give us one or two examples so we can understand what you mean.

DIVVER: If we took him from his place of confinement to court or a restaurant, he would never get out of a car unless we got out first. He would never walk in a door unless a detective went in, he would stay right up close.

Q: Would he make it a habit to stay away from openings, somebody might take a bead on him?

DIVVER: He was very careful of windows and doors.

Q: Would he at times call the attention of some of his guards to something that looked suspicious to him, that they should check?

DIVVER: Very often.

Watchful and wary, Reles's survival instincts were constantly on high alert; his radar was always scanning his surroundings for potentially life-threatening situations. Divver testified about a telling incident that took place when Reles was in the hospital. Though he'd been admitted under an alias, Reles knew that such a flimsy ruse wouldn't throw a savvy hit man off his trail. One night, a guard posted in his hospital room received a phone call from home. Reles went into panic mode. He phoned Divver with a frenzied lecture: If the Mob found out about the call, then it would know where the guard was posted—and it could safely assume that Reles was there, too. A chill went up Divver's spine as Reles's words sank in. He immediately added extra security and cashiered the guard who'd caused the ruckus. Silver was struck by the extent of Reles's anxiety. "He was in fear that the Mob might raid the hospital?" he asked. "That the wrong people might get the information," Divver answered gravely.

Divver also testified that Reles never felt completely safe, even when he was in the fortified squealers' suite. Fearful of being poisoned, he expected the guards to act as his official tasters; he would wait until they drank from a pot of coffee before pouring himself a cup. He would also carefully inspect his food for evidence of poison, and he insisted on having the same hotel waiters bring his meals to him each day.

Frank Bals's testimony about Reles's hypervigilance was equally compelling:

Q: From your observations of him and what he would say to you concerning his worries and his fears, you are still convinced, are you not, that the only thing he didn't want to do was go into the outside world?
BALS: I am convinced of that and nothing has changed my opinion.

Bals related a story about taking a plane trip with Reles to Los Angeles, where he was scheduled to testify before a grand jury investigating organized crime boss Benjamin "Bugsy" Siegel. "His demeanor and conduct with me," Bals said of Reles, "would indicate that he wanted to stay as close to a policeman as possible." Silver pressed for specifics:

Q: What you are trying to tell me is that he was scared of the outside world, his kind of world, his [former] friends?
BALS: He certainly was. On one occasion he wouldn't leave the hotel because [he believed] they were going to bomb the plane. We had to take him to the plane.
Q: You say you had to take him to the plane, how did you do it?
BALS: Almost bodily.
Q: He was afraid of the plane ride or afraid that somebody had planted a bomb?
BALS: He was afraid of the Mob.
Q: He not only was afraid to go to the plane, but also concerned that somebody would plant a bomb on the plane to get rid of everybody?

Bals: That's right, that's all he talked about.

Q: The Mob would go to any extremes to get him?

Bals: That's right.

The former guards testified that Reles had no illusions about the fact that fleeing the Half Moon Hotel would be tantamount to signing his own death warrant. Silver asked Victor Robbins if Reles ever discussed bolting. "He always said he wouldn't have a chance if he did escape," Robbins remembered. "He said, 'I'd be killed by the Mob.'" Harvey McLaughlin told Silver of the special security arrangements Reles demanded before going to the hotel's barber shop: "He would want you to sit directly in line with the chair so nobody could draw a bead from across the way. He would say 'You are here to protect me. I am not going to take a chance on getting killed.'"

Clearly, the witnesses were of a single mind: Reles knew that the only way he could stay out of the Mob's crosshairs was to remain in the Half Moon Hotel. His fear of underworld retaliation was all-consuming. And yet, Silver mused, could something have driven Reles into making a bid for freedom? Die-hard supporters of the official story were continually speculating about what his possible motives would have been for trying to flee. So Silver decided to take a closer look at several of the escape-attempt scenarios they'd put forth over the years.

One scenario that began circulating shortly after Reles's death suggested that he had a large stash of money hidden somewhere in Brooklyn. After his escape, he planned to recover it, then join his wife and two children to begin a new life somewhere far from his old stomping grounds. It seemed like a plausible theory, but Silver was able to rule it out because of the security setup that was in place in 1941. He found that Reles's family was under constant police guard: A squad car was parked in front of their home at all times, and Mrs. Reles's bodyguards accompanied her everywhere she went. It would have been impossible for Reles to meet up with his family as part of an escape plan. And relocating would have been futile because, as Reles himself said, the Mob could—and would—find him anywhere on the planet.

Another scenario involved Lepke's trial for the murder of Joseph

Rosen. (The trial, which had begun in September 1941, was nearing its end by mid-November.) Here, the speculation was that Reles lost his nerve at the thought of testifying against his onetime benefactor and decided instead to beat a hasty retreat. However, this scenario died a quick death after Silver spoke with Burton Turkus, who prosecuted Lepke. Turkus explained that Allie Tannenbaum, not Reles, was the critical witness against Lepke, because only Tannenbaum could supply the testimony of a non-accomplice. Since Reles had been in prison at the time of Joseph Rosen's death, he was considered an unimportant witness in the case. As for Reles losing his nerve at the idea of facing Lepke in court, Turkus believed just the opposite was true: "Reles was looking forward to this appearance, just so that he could publicly display his past intimacy with the mighty Lepke."

Silver also ran the fear-of-facing-Lepke scenario past Hyman Barshay, Lepke's lead defense attorney at the Rosen trial. Barshay agreed with Turkus that there were no expectations whatsoever that Reles would testify to anything injurious to Lepke. When Silver asked Barshay what he thought about the official story of Reles's death, he got an earful: "As far as the escape theory was concerned," Silver wrote in a memo, "Barshay said that it was ridiculous. He said Reles knew that if he escaped, the cops would shoot him on sight, and if the cops didn't, members of the underworld would. In his opinion, interests that felt Reles' continued existence would be very inimical to them somehow did away with Reles."

Another scenario involved Reles's immunity deal. Was it possible that by the fall of 1941, Reles began to worry that O'Dwyer considered him a well that had run dry? That O'Dwyer was planning somehow to renege on the deal, leaving him vulnerable to a long stretch in prison— or worse? Might his concern have been heightened by a widely read *New York Times* editorial that asked if he should be "allowed to save his life on any terms"? Was Reles afraid that the editorial had changed some minds in the public and the DA's office toward his grant of immunity? Silver was surprised to learn that the late Captain John McGowan, architect of the escape-attempt theory, believed that this was the reason Reles tried to flee. Silver questioned Lieutenant Joseph Donovan, the captain's deputy in 1941, about McGowan's thinking:

Q: Was there any information that came to you or McGowan explaining why Reles wanted to escape in light of the fact that he was scared out of his wits of the outside world[?]

DONOVAN: We had come to the conclusion that Reles felt he would have to do a bit [serve jail time], and that his life would be in jeopardy in prison.

Q: By November 12th, it is your idea that Reles began to realize that he wasn't getting out of the situation without some prison term?

DONOVAN: That's right.

Q: And that if he went to prison his life there would not be much safer than if he was walking around the streets with the Mob after him?

DONOVAN: That's right.

When Silver put this theory to the test, however, it simply disintegrated. Elwood Divver, for one, testified that Reles "seemed to have an optimistic view of his future so far as what might happen to him and he felt satisfied." Frank Bals was quizzed about whether Reles was concerned about what O'Dwyer had in store for him:

Q: How long before he died did he begin to worry and complain about what [O'Dwyer] was going to do to him when it was all over?

BALS: I don't recall his complaining about that . . .

Q: Do you mean that he never expressed a concern to you as to what ultimately would happen to him?

BALS: I don't recall any at this time.

There was a wealth of evidence that Reles still had more to offer investigators. While poring over old files in the DA's office, Silver found dozens of investigations, prompted by Reles's revelations, that were pending at the time of his death. And it wasn't piddling stuff, either—many of these cases involved major organized crime figures. For example, Reles gave O'Dwyer information linking Joe Adonis, a high-echelon New York mobster with significant political clout, to a double murder dating back to the mid-1930s. Reles explained that the victims, Joseph Biunde and his wife, were murdered to prevent them from revealing the vast sums Adonis had extorted from the taxicab industry. Had he lived, Reles would have testified at trial that Adonis gave the order to murder the Biundes.

Silver also found letters to O'Dwyer from lawmen seeking to question Reles about Mob activities in their jurisdictions. Though O'Dwyer granted a handful of these requests, he was stingy when it came to many prosecutors who, he feared, might steal his glory. Case in point: John Harlem Amen, the special prosecutor appointed in 1938 to probe graft in Brooklyn. The DA routinely rejected his requests to ask Reles about payoffs to political figures and high-ranking members of the NYPD. "For months I tried to get to see Reles alone," Amen groused, "but O'Dwyer kept him under lock and key." On the few occasions when O'Dwyer relented, the questioning "was always in O'Dwyer's office and in front of O'Dwyer himself. It was something of a farce. You could see right away that Reles was afraid to talk. I was never able to get him to tell me the names of the officials to whom the Mob paid the protection money."

Judge Matthew F. Troy, who was overseeing Amen's work, had sharp words for the DA: "I charge that O'Dwyer has failed to prosecute political fixers who arranged for the protection of the killers in Murder, Inc. He has prevented Reles from giving Amen information about the protection set-up. Reles can name the politicians and political fixers and can give the necessary evidence to put them in jail." Despite the reprimand, O'Dwyer continued to withhold his cooperation.

■■■

Silver also checked out speculation that Reles's death had been a suicide; rumors that the prize canary had taken his own life made periodic reappearances in the press since 1941. For example, the February 1944 edition of *Life* magazine carried a retrospective on the life of Lepke, who was awaiting execution at Sing Sing. The article suggested that Reles, tortured by guilt over being a snitch, killed himself because "the strain was too much," and that he was truly remorseful about "sending his fellow men-at-arms [*sic*] to the death house."

Like the escape-attempt theories, the suicide scenario fell apart when Silver scrutinized it more carefully. Although Reles had never been given a psychological exam, there was much anecdotal evidence that he wasn't suicidal. When Reles's guards were questioned on November 12, 1941, they agreed that he hadn't displayed any mood swings or other peculiar behavior in the days before his death.

George Govans, the night bellhop at the Half Moon Hotel, was one of the last people to see Reles alive. Govans told Silver that at about 1:30 a.m. on November 12, Reles called the front desk and told the night manager to send up a cash voucher for ten dollars. When Govans entered the squealers' suite, Reles snatched the voucher—which required a signature from one of the guards—and signed it with a fictitious name as a practical joke. Govans distinctly recalled that Reles "was in a very good mood." When Govans's boss saw the bogus signature, he sent the bellhop back to the suite to straighten things out. Reles was absolutely delighted with this bit of mischief: "I see my signature is no good," he chortled. (Interestingly, this bit of levity on Reles's part took place just a few hours after his wife's unpleasant visit.)

Another major problem with the suicide theory, Silver concluded, was Reles's enormous ego. Former guard Harvey McLaughlin was just one of the witnesses who doubted that Reles would have taken his own life: "I don't think Abe was that type," he testified. "He was an egocentric type, very conceited. He used to think that he was one of the cleverest guys in the business. I don't imagine the guy would kill himself."

Lastly, Silver reckoned that if Reles had wanted to kill himself, there were at least three simple ways he could have done it: by hanging himself; by jumping out of his window (without first taking the time to put together a makeshift rope); or by using a service revolver snatched from one of the guards.

■■■

Though his staff thought it was a waste of time, Silver felt obligated to consider Bals's "peek-a-boo theory." Did Reles die from a prank gone haywire? Did he intend to lower himself to the fifth floor of the hotel, then return to the squealers' suite to surprise the guards? Bals, still smarting from his Kefauver ordeal, didn't put up much resistance as Silver took apart his crackpot notion:

Q: Isn't it true that you have said that Reles was a thorough physical coward?

BALS: Yes, that's right.

Q: Isn't that inconsistent with any theory that he would risk hanging five floors from a window just to play games with the cops?

BALS: When I gave the opinion that he was a coward, I meant to convey that he is a brave man when the odds are with him, but if he had even chances he wouldn't take them. He was a man that commits a dozen murders and there isn't one that the man he killed had a chance for his life.

Q: Knowing him as you did, you admit that he was a pretty careful planner about his murders?

BALS: That's right, he took no chances.

Q: In light of that do you think he would suspend himself five floors from the ground unless he knew pretty much in advance that he could get into that [fifth-floor] window?

BALS: I can't answer that. How would I know that? I assume from the physical evidence that's the only place he could get to.

Q: How would he find out, Captain, that the room beneath him was unoccupied?

BALS: That I can't answer.

In the course of weighing the peek-a-boo theory, Silver came across a new twist in the mystery of the vacant room. Alexander Lysberg, who was working at the hotel's front desk, testified that sometime after 11:00 p.m. on November 11, 1941, he received a call from the squealers' suite "asking if there was anybody in the hotel they should know about, and whether or not the suite below and adjacent room [524] were occupied. I told them 523 was vacant and that the adjoining room was occupied by people we knew." Was Reles the caller? Inexplicably, Silver didn't ask Lysberg if he recognized the voice, and Lysberg didn't volunteer a name. But the fact that the caller asked "if there was anybody in the hotel they should know about" suggests that it was one of the guards making routine checks on the identity of the hotel's guests—part of Captain Bals's security protocol.

■■■

Silver had debunked the escape, suicide, and prank scenarios, but a disquieting question now loomed larger than ever: How did the makeshift rope fit into the case? If Reles had no reason to flee—if the very thought of freedom terrified him—then what use would he have had for an escape device? Something just didn't add up. Hoping to nail down the provenance of the makeshift rope, Silver decided to have it examined by a crime lab. Normally, he would have called on the NYPD, but the appearance of a conflict of interest would be too strong. So Silver retained the services of the FBI crime lab in Washington, DC.

On May 7, 1951, Silver hand-delivered the makeshift rope to the FBI lab. After explaining the escape-attempt theory to the criminalists, he asked them to: (1) inspect the knotted bedsheets for signs—such as "strain or alteration" of the fabric—that they'd held Reles's suspended weight, suggesting that they may have been used as a makeshift rope; (2) process the bedsheets for fingerprints; (3) inspect the wire tied to the bedsheets for traces of paint from the radiator pipe to which it was allegedly attached;

The makeshift rope at FBI lab (photographed in 1951). [NYC Municipal Archives]

and (4) determine whether Reles's weight (160 pounds) could have caused the wire to unwind from the radiator pipe.

One week later, Silver received the test results. They were not encouraging. The criminalists checked the bedsheets "in the vicinity of the wire and the area on each side of the knot for evidence of strain or alteration of the woven construction," but found nothing suspicious. A visual examination of the sheets didn't turn up any fingerprints, and the FBI warned that using chemicals to develop prints would be "impractical" due to the "coarse weave" of the sheets. Microscopic inspection of the wire failed to reveal "any significant foreign paint deposits" that might have come from the radiator pipe.

In order to determine the weight needed to cause the wire to unwind, the FBI performed tensile force tests, also known as pull tests. These tests were flawed from the outset. First, the criminalists used wire that was similar, not identical, to the wire on the makeshift rope (identical wire wasn't available because Captain McGowan hadn't bothered to keep any). Second, Silver failed to give the criminalists the diameter of the pipe, so they were forced to guess the size. After winding the wire around the pipe six times (another guess), a tensile stress machine was used to pull the free end of the wire away from the pipe. The test was performed three times, and the wire unwound at twenty-five, thirty, and fifty pounds of pull, respectively. Since Reles weighed 160 pounds, it seemed as though the results were at least consistent with the official story. But the lab added a disclaimer that all but nullified the results: "No conclusion could be reached in the determination of the amount of pull necessary to pull the wire free from the radiator as it is not known how the wire had been attached to the pipe, whether the wire had been tied or knotted, or what the angle or distance was from the radiator pipe to the edge of the window frame."

In short, none of the tests the FBI performed linked the makeshift rope to Reles or to the escape-attempt theory.

On June 27, Silver penned a follow-up letter to the lab, admitting that the test results had raised "a number of new problems." He asked if there were any marks on the wire consistent with its "being hung over a window and pulled" by a weight of 160 pounds. Silver then made two unwise decisions, both with irreversible consequences. First, he gave the lab permission to untie the knot in the bedsheets so that the fabric in that area could be chemically tested for fingerprints, even though the lab had warned that the material wouldn't respond to those tests. Second, he asked for more pull tests—this time using the *actual wire* still attached to the makeshift rope.

On July 9, the FBI reported that "there were no marks on the wire which could be identified as having been made by attaching one end to a radiator and hanging the other end out a window supporting a load of 160 pounds." Not a single fingerprint was found as a result of chemical testing in the area of the now untied knot. Lastly, three pull tests using "a portion" of the original wire were carried out. Even though the test was supposed to establish the force needed to *unwind* the wire from a pipe, the criminalists allowed the tensile stress machine to pull the wire until it broke apart—at approximately 130 pounds of pull. And once again, the criminalists added a major disclaimer to the report: "It is not possible to determine what the exact tensile strength of the wire was at the time of the death of Abe Reles in November 1941." It was déjà vu all over again: There was still nothing to link the makeshift rope to Reles.

The tests had settled nothing, and Silver never contacted the crime lab again; in fact, FBI director J. Edgar Hoover had to send him a letter reminding him to retrieve the makeshift rope from the lab. Thanks to Silver's shortsightedness, there wasn't much left to retrieve. The bedsheets had been separated, then badly damaged by the needless use of fingerprint-developing chemicals. The wire had been untied and cut into pieces. For all practical purposes, the single most important piece of physical evidence in the Reles case no longer existed.

■■■

Was the makeshift rope nothing more than a prop designed to mask something sinister? Forensic science wasn't able to provide an answer, but maybe common sense can. "The Reles stamp was not there," former Murder, Inc., prosecutor Burton Turkus said of the device. "Reles was handier with a rope than a gaucho of the pampas or a deck-hand on a four-master. Yet the impression created by the death scene would have you believe that, risking his own neck, Reles tied a knot which came undone almost as soon as his weight pulled against it. Or, that after all the successful getaways he had blue-printed, he prepared no better for his own flight than the flimsy bedsheet rope which came apart on the first try. Not Reles!"

Rose Reles, Abe's widow, was one of the most eagerly awaited witnesses of the new investigation. She was the only person alive who knew what had taken place during her turbulent visit with her husband at the Half Moon Hotel just hours before his death. As Silver would find out, however, getting information out of Rose was not easy. It shouldn't have come as a surprise. Since that fateful day in 1941, the widow had tried desperately to distance herself from the shadow of her late husband. A few months after he died, she asked a judge to restore her maiden name, arguing that the surname Reles was looked upon with "disdain, contempt and scorn," and that going through life with it was an "unwarranted hardship." The judge granted her request. Rose later remarried and—with her two children by Abe in tow—left New York City. When her new neighbors learned her true identity, they couldn't resist asking about November 12, 1941. "I would answer that I never want to discuss it," Rose told Silver in disgust.

Silver was sympathetic to Rose's plight. He even tried to shield her from pushy reporters by not disclosing where she now lived. And when she returned to Brooklyn to testify, he kept the date and location of her appearance under wraps. To show her appreciation, Rose did nothing but make his life difficult. She caused him grief about even the most mundane matters:

Q: When did you marry Reles?
Rose: I don't remember when.
Q: How long before he died did you marry him?
Rose: I can't remember.
Q: Were you married to him a year, two years—he was the father of your children.
Rose: Sure.
Q: Then you must have been married to him at least seven years before he died?

ROSE: Yes.

Q: How long after you married Abe did you have your first baby?

ROSE: About a year and a half.

Q: Which means you married him ten or eleven years before he died?

ROSE: I imagine so.

Rose put on a babe-in-the-woods act whenever she was asked about her husband's bloodstained past. Her behavior caused the mild-mannered Silver to lose his cool:

Q: How did you think he was making a living all those years?

ROSE: He was a bookmaker and a shylock, and then he went into the luncheonette business and gambling.

Q: You never knew he was a pretty tough guy, that he killed people in his day—you are sure of that?

ROSE: I am almost sure.

Q: Didn't you know, as everybody in Brownsville knew, that Abie Reles was the toughest guy in Brownsville? You didn't know that?

ROSE: I never felt that way.

Q: I didn't ask how you felt. I said, didn't you know that Abe Reles was considered one of the toughest guys in Brownsville?

ROSE: How would you know something? Is somebody supposed to tell it to you?

Q: All you knew was that he was a bookmaker and a loan shark, and that's all he was doing?

ROSE: That's right. I never knew.

Q: I am through proving things to you and you saying "I don't remember." You can go to the Grand Jury and tell them the facts and we will let the Grand Jury determine whether you perjured yourself.

Fearing that she may have pushed Silver too far, Rose tried to mollify him with an insipid story about how Reles kept her in the dark: "He would buy up every single paper in circulation, and when he would get through reading them, I used to pick them up and try to find out why—but I could never find anything in them because he would take out pieces and I could not find the next page."

Spinning his wheels with this line of questioning, Silver jumped ahead to Rose's last tête-à-tête with her husband. It was the moment for which everyone had been waiting. But the widow already had her guard up:

Q: How long did you spend with Reles that evening?

ROSE: I was there a very short time. I just came and went.

Q: Would it refresh your recollection if I told you that almost everybody that was there states that you were there for a number of hours that evening?

ROSE: They were just guessing. I don't know how anybody can say it.

Q: As I told you before, I want to be helpful to you so far as making this as easy as I can for you and for your kids, but I'm not going to do it if I feel you are not cooperating with me. Our information is that you were there at that time for a much longer visit than you usually were there.

ROSE: No, that's not true; that is absolutely not true.

Of course, it *was* true. "You were there almost three hours," Silver shot back. "I have checked the records." Feigning remorse, Rose replied: "I didn't mean to lie."

According to Rose, her husband spent the entire three hours whining about his poor health: "I didn't talk. He did the talking. He told me that he had been in the hospital and how sick he was, and that's what he talked about." Silver didn't believe that even a self-centered creep like Reles could be that long-winded about his ailments, yet Rose continued to insist that it was true. Again, Silver lost his cool: "I'm asking you again so my conscience will be clear," he warned. "Is there anything he told you that night that, in the light of subsequent events, now has meaning? Now, what's your answer?" Rose was adamant: "No, there wasn't; I'm very sure."

Then, out of the blue, Rose announced that she would reveal "the true reason" she went to the Half Moon that Tuesday night. Silver leaned forward in anticipation. The reason, she said, was to get Reles to sign divorce papers. It was a bombshell—until Rose changed her story just seconds later. There were no actual divorce papers, only a single, blank sheet of paper. Silver, his eyes glazing over, struggled to make sense of Rose's revelation:

> Q: I am trying to get this straight. Did you ask him to sign a blank piece of paper?
>
> ROSE: I told him I would write in all the particulars. He would not even hear of it. I didn't bother talking to him any more.
>
> Q: What particulars were you going to put there that you wanted him to sign?
>
> ROSE: Just that that was his signature for a divorce. That when I'd get started, I'd have his signature and that's all there was to it.
>
> Q: In other words—see if I get this straight—you wanted him to sign a piece of paper which, in substance, said that if you wanted a divorce . . . that this was sort of a consent that he agreed to it—is that what you meant?
>
> ROSE: Yes, it was that way . . .
>
> Q: Well, did he take it calmly?
>
> ROSE: Well, no—he looked at me as though sick, and he said: "At a time like this, you would do a thing like that?" and I don't think I went into it any further.
>
> Q: Did you get his signature?
>
> ROSE: No.

Silver's patience was evaporating. "Is there anything that you can tell me," he asked the widow sternly, "that would help me to determine whether Abe Reles went out the window of his own volition or whether he was pushed by somebody?" Rose seemed to have been waiting for this moment. Though she didn't give a damn about how her husband died, she *did* want Silver and his prying questions to go away so that she could slip back into anonymity. She knew, however, that as long as the investigation continued, she would remain in the spotlight. Immature and arrogant, Rose believed that she could single-handedly bring the entire probe to a swift conclusion. How? By giving Silver an answer—better yet, an anecdote he couldn't disprove—that would seem to "solve" the case. If she even remotely hinted at foul play, there would be no end to her woes. But if she suggested that her husband died trying to escape, she thought, her nightmare might end quickly.

"I'm going to tell you now," she began conspiratorily.

Rose proceeded to spin another fantastic tale. At some point in his illustrious career, Reles had been hiding out from the cops at the home of mobster Louis Capone. One morning, Reles suddenly showed up at his own house and began pounding on the door. "I asked him what was the idea [*sic*]," Rose testified. "He said he just wanted to see us. I remember I thought he was crazy." When Capone came to retrieve his missing houseguest, he asked Rose: "Do you know what Abe did? He tied a bed sheet to something and went down it." This yarn was Rose's way of saying: *You see, Mr. Silver, there's no big mystery here. Abe had done it all before—right down to tying bedsheets together to make a rope. Now please, please, call off your investigation.*

Obviously, Silver was not about to call it quits based on Rose's cockamamie tale. Much to her dismay, he began punching holes in the story:

Q: You don't know that Abe got out of that house with the aid of
    a sheet, other than what somebody said to you, is that right?
ROSE: Yes, that's right.
Q: At any time in his lifetime, other than that occasion, had Abe
    ever tried to do anything like that?
ROSE: No—not that I know of.

Silver got Rose to admit that Capone's home was only two stories high. Why in the world, he asked her, would Reles have bothered to use a makeshift rope at all? Apparently Rose hadn't anticipated that simple question; she sat silent and stone-faced. Silver then pointed out that the story couldn't be corroborated: Louis Capone had been executed in 1944, and no one else knew about the alleged incident. Nevertheless, Rose tried to hold together her rapidly crumbling story. When she testified one month later, she added a detail that just happened to match a key part of the escape-attempt theory: "He [Reles] tied a sheet *to the radiator* and just went down the sheet."

Rose believed that she'd knocked one out of the park with the Capone story: "I think I am the only one who solved this mystery," she crowed. Silver had an entirely different take: Rose would continue throwing one preposterous tale after another against the wall, hoping that one would stick. At the end of her third and final day of testimony, Silver had to admit that the witness for whom he'd entertained such high hopes had turned out to be a train wreck.

■■■

After he slammed into a brick wall named Rose Reles, Silver turned to the only other person who might know something about the tempestuous final meeting of Rose and Abe Reles: Frank Bals. It was Bals who had questioned Mrs. Reles late in the day on November 12, 1941, after having her shuttled around Brooklyn in an effort to keep her from learning of her husband's fate. Silver knew that Bals hadn't kept any record of the questioning, so he instinctively lowered his expectations. Bals didn't disappoint:

> Q: Did you question her concerning what she and Reles had spoken about during her last visit?
> BALS: There is no doubt that I did.
> Q: Do you know what the conversation was?
> BALS: No, I don't.
> Q: Did you suggest to Mrs. Reles that he had been trying to escape?
> BALS: I may have.
> Q: Do you remember what answers she gave you?
> BALS: No, I don't.

Q: There is nothing whatever you can remember about your talk
    with her on the day of his death?

BALS: No, there isn't.

■■■

There was a brief but exciting moment when Silver thought he might
still get the lowdown on the final meeting of Abe and Rose Reles. A tipster passed along the tantalizing news that a listening device had been
planted in Reles's room during his stay at the Half Moon Hotel. Elwood
Divver, Frank Bals's deputy, conceded that a special Dictaphone had
indeed been secreted in Reles's room "in order to check up on whether
or not he was communicating with anyone outside of the proper
authorities." Divver said that the "listening post" for the bug was probably located below the squealers' suite—perhaps in room 524. He was
sure that Reles had never learned about the bug, and that it would have
been removed when it failed to produce anything of value.

Silver had his investigators scour the files of the Brooklyn DA and
the NYPD for any record of the hidden microphone, but the searches
proved fruitless.

Frank Bals was of little help. "That could be, but I can't even think
of it now," he said of the purported bug, though he did concede that if
one had been planted, "it was most likely at my direction." Unwilling to
drop this important matter, Silver tried to refresh Bals's memory:

Q: If I told you the manager of the hotel [Paul Fulton, who "dis-
    covered" the window tampering in Room 523] told me that
    he listened to recordings of conversations in Reles's room,
    does that help you to remember?

BALS: No, it does not help me, but I would say that most likely he
    is right because he would have more reason to remember it
    than I have.

Why in the world would hotel manager Fulton have "more reason to
remember" an eavesdropping operation involving a Mob turncoat than
the police official who ordered it? Try as he might, Silver couldn't wrap

his mind around Bals's response; attempting to follow the captain's logic was like chasing someone through a maze of funhouse mirrors.

But a much more important question loomed over the proceedings: Why was Paul Fulton permitted to listen to the secret recordings in the first place? What exactly was his relationship with the police officers who'd been responsible for protecting Reles? Unfortunately, Silver never asked—and nobody volunteered an answer.

Chapter 14
Tin Badge Cops

Imagine a bunch of hard-core criminals living with a group of police officers for a year. It may sound like some sort of bizarre sociological experiment, but it was real life for the Murder, Inc., canaries and their guards at the Half Moon Hotel. Three shifts of five guards each lived with Reles and his three fellow snitches around the clock. To hear Bals tell it, the bad guys and the good guys lived together in perfect harmony. No one could verify this eyebrow-raising claim because the captain never allowed the press into the squealers' suite. (In banning the media, Bals cited his concern that an overzealous reporter might put lives in jeopardy by revealing details of the security arrangements.) So how had Bals maintained harmony between the two camps? Medication? Hypnosis? According to the captain, he simply ordered the guards to provide the squealers with "a lot of humoring" and to "keep them in the best of spirits at all times."

The former guards vividly remembered Bals's edict about how to treat the squealers.

"Our job was to humor them and to keep them in a good mood," James Boyle told Ed Silver.

"Keep them happy. That's the word we got," Victor Robbins testified.

According to Harvey McLaughlin, Bals said that Reles and his three colleagues were "under a strain because they are very highly wanted by the underworld. You will have to give them a little leeway."

Silver wondered: Precisely what did "a lot of humoring" mean? How far were the guards supposed to go to keep the squealers in a "good mood" or "happy"? How much was "a little leeway" when dealing with the stool pigeons? Was it possible that the humoring led to a laxity about keeping order, which in turn might have contributed to Reles's death?

Most of the humoring, Silver found, was innocent enough. For example, if one of the squealers requested a particular magazine or newspaper, a guard would pick up a copy for him. If the request was for a particular meal, a guard would try to arrange for it with the Half Moon Hotel's management. Or if one of the canaries was especially tense over an upcoming court appearance, a guard might suggest a friendly game of cards to ease the strain.

But there was also a dark side to the humoring edict. While studying a transcript of Lepke's 1941 murder trial, Silver was astonished to find that the guards allowed Sholem Bernstein to run an extortion scheme right out of the squealers' suite! Not only did the guards look the other way, but they were also the ones who mailed the extortion letters to the intended targets. Even Lepke's lawyer, who tried to discredit Bernstein on the witness stand, had a hard time believing it: "You wrote that while you were in custody in the Half Moon?" he'd asked during the trial, waving a threatening missive written on hotel stationery. "Yes, sir," Bernstein had answered matter-of-factly. "With a guard beside me. He seen it, sir." Bernstein testified that he'd sent at least four or five similar extortion letters.

Silver got copies of the remaining Bernstein letters from the law firm that had defended Lepke. He was stunned by the way Bernstein brazenly exploited his position as a state's witness to put teeth into his demands for money. One letter, written to a former partner in crime named Ben Glass, read in part:

> Why don't you get wise? Do you know what I can do to you? I could have you pinched tomorrow if I want to. Don't kid yourself. I'm going to give you EXACTLY ONE WEEK to give my wife $200 and five dollars every week. If you don't, I'm going to put you in [here] with me. My wife gives me a visit next week, and if she tells me you didn't give it to her, as true as GOD you will be right [here] with me.

Glass didn't pay up, so an irate Bernstein fired off another letter hiking his price and ratcheting up his threats:

> Now I'm raising it to $300.00 and 5 [dollars] every week. Today is Sunday—if my wife don't get that money when she comes to

visit me, as true as my mother (may she rest in peace), I'm going to make so much trouble for you that $300 will be spit.

Much to Ed Silver's dismay, the meddlesome Walter Winchell obtained a copy of one of Bernstein's letters. Winchell immediately printed excerpts from it in his *New York Daily Mirror* column. In the same column, he needled Silver's boss, Miles McDonald, about why Bernstein hadn't been charged with extortion for penning the threats. (Winchell should have asked the question of William O'Dwyer, who was the DA at the time the letters were written.) Despite his grandstanding, Winchell never received an answer from McDonald. And although Bernstein was never charged with extortion, he never collected a cent from the folks he'd threatened, either.

Captain Bals's humor-the-squealers order also meant that if a guard were to be mistreated, physically or verbally, by any of the squealers, he was expected to turn the other cheek. Here Reles takes center stage: He exploited this situation for all it was worth. Reles delighted in playing cruel pranks on his guards, only to remind them with a sneer that they were not permitted to retaliate in any way. Make no mistake: Reles's pranks were not misguided attempts to break the monotony in the suite. They were a way of showing his utter contempt for the cops.

"Abe was very abusive, very fresh," former guard Harvey McLaughlin recalled resentfully. "He would do things that you wouldn't take from anybody else. He would throw a wet roll of toilet paper at you and think it was a big joke." Spooning heaps of pepper into an unsuspecting guard's coffee or inserting a lit match into one of his shoes were two of Reles's signature pranks. Vile behavior was another one of his specialties: "He had a habit of spitting in his hand and showing it to you, streams of blood and everything, and he was given to exposing himself," McLaughlin testified.

Reles did everything he could to get under the guards' skin, to provoke them. He would phone an off-duty guard at 4:30 a.m. and awaken him from a sound sleep. As the startled man's heart was racing a mile a minute, Reles put on his most official-sounding voice: "We are making a check. Just look out the window and see if the street light is lit, will you?" Another time, Reles placed a 2:00 a.m. call to the hotel room of a newly married guard. "This is your friend, Kid Twist," he said in his uniquely smarmy way. "I just wanted to see how you're enjoying your honeymoon."

Reles also kept up a steady stream of verbal insults. He ridiculed the guards as "tin badge" cops. "What are you guys going to get out of this?" he'd sneer. "You know what's going to happen. All the murderers are going to go free and the cops will go to jail." He took great pleasure in reminding the guards that they were duty-bound to take a bullet for him if necessary: "That's what you're getting paid for," he'd taunt.

The guards' morale sank under Reles's relentless abuse. They came to loathe the squealers' suite detail. Harvey McLaughlin spoke for his brethren when he testified: "I don't know anybody that liked the job. We wanted to get out of there."

So why did they stay? The principal reason, Silver learned, was that Captain Bals had dangled the prospect of promotions in front of them. (The patrolmen were hoping to make detective, while the detectives were aiming for a jump in pay grade.) According to McLaughlin, the captain had promised that when the assignment ended, "you will be recommended for it [promotion]." Bals's promise was an empty one. Not a single guard who paid his dues in the squealers' suite ever received a promotion.

Once he'd uncovered proof that life in the suite was hardly idyllic, it wasn't much of a leap for Silver to question Bals's sunny assurances that the security procedures ran like clockwork. He began to focus on the guards' activities on the night Reles plunged to his death. When they were interrogated in 1941, the guards had insisted that they'd made periodic bed checks of all four snitches during the overnight hours of November 11–12. But if that were the case, how could Reles have gone out the window without the guards knowing it? This was sure to be a taboo subject, and Silver fully expected to run into the police "code of silence" when he began asking about it. As it turned out, however, he caught an enormously lucky break.

It happened during Silver's questioning of former guard Harvey McLaughlin. McLaughlin began venting over some of the resentment he'd been holding in for more than a decade concerning Bals's order to humor the squealers, Reles's demeaning conduct, and the guards' frustration over their predicament. He continued to unburden himself as the questioning went on. But even Silver seemed to be caught off-guard when the dam finally burst:

Q: Did you have a regular routine as to how often you would make rounds to see if the men were safe?

McLAUGHLIN: No, sir.

Q: You mean that nobody gave you instructions that you go every half hour or twenty minutes to take a look around during the night?

McLAUGHLIN: We worked it out amongst ourselves. There was always somebody strolling around by the windows or looking out at the Boardwalk. *As far as being at a certain point at a certain time, there was nothing like that.*

Just like that, a key tenet of the escape-attempt theory imploded. The official story had Reles going out the window, *between bed checks*, sometime between 7:00 a.m. and 7:10 a.m. If the bed checks weren't performed at regular intervals, if nobody looked in on the squealers, then Reles's death plunge could have happened much earlier. Perhaps even at 4:30 a.m., when Half Moon employees Alfred Wolfarth and George Govans, along with NYPD officers Charles Burns and Thomas Doyle, heard a loud thud coming from the east side of the building as they sat in the lobby. Not only did McLaughlin's admission deal a crushing blow to the official story, it also gave Silver a tool with which to force the other guards into realizing that the jig was up.

As for his own actions on that fateful night, McLaughlin conceded that he may have catnapped. He became flustered when asked what his fellow guards were up to:

Q: Did you see them up and around or were they asleep?

McLAUGHLIN: Not asleep; none of them were asleep.

Q: You don't know, do you?

McLAUGHLIN: I didn't look to see if they were asleep. No, I can't say for sure.

Experienced prosecutor that he was, Silver wasted no time in confronting the other former guards with McLaughlin's revelations. Apparently this was done off the record, because by the time the guards formally testified, it was clear that they knew Silver was on to them. Francisco Tempone was the first of the guards to come clean:

Q: Prior to learning that Abe Reles was no longer in the suite, what were you doing?

TEMPONE: I was sleeping in Room 628.

Q: When did you go to sleep?

TEMPONE: I don't know the definite hour.

Q: Can you tell me whether it was before or after midnight?

TEMPONE: After midnight . . .

Q: Would it be fair to state it was for at least a matter of some hours you were asleep?

TEMPONE: Yes, sir.

Q: Was there anyone else in bed in Room 628?

TEMPONE: There was another man in the room, but I don't know if he was in bed or not.

Q: What is the name of that man?

TEMPONE: Detective Robbins—he was a detective at that time . . .

Q: During the course of the night you at no time visited Room 623, is that right?

TEMPONE: That's right.

Tempone described how the guards conspired to cover up their negligence:

Q: After Detective Robbins returned to the room following his visit to the roof where the body of Reles lay, did you and your brother officers hold any conference concerning the occurrence?

TEMPONE: Yes.

Q: Was there anything said about whether or not it would be asserted that you police officers had visited the rooms at twenty minute intervals, and on such intervals did see Reles in the room?

TEMPONE: That's right.

Q: All five of you reached an agreement to say that one of you visited the suite every twenty minutes?

TEMPONE: That's right, sir.

Q: And that, of course, was not the truth?

TEMPONE: That's right.

Q: Subsequently, you were questioned by Assistant District Attorney Heffernan, is that correct?

TEMPONE: Yes, sir.

Q: In answering his questions, did you make your answer consistent with the story that you and your brother officers agreed to tell?

TEMPONE: Yes, sir.

The turkey shoot continued with James Boyle. "I moped around from place to place," Boyle said about the night in question. Between 3:00 a.m. and 3:30 a.m., he went into room 620 (the guards' command post) to make a pot of coffee. At some point, Reles appeared. "He was outside the door, standing there," Boyle testified. "I asked him did he want a cup of coffee. He said 'No.' Then he went toward the parlor room or his room."

Q: When and where did you next see Abe Reles?

BOYLE: The next time I saw Reles was when I saw his body on the extension roof of the Half Moon Hotel.

Q: So that at no time in between the two points in time you have just stated—when you offered him a cup of coffee and when you saw his body—did you see Abe Reles?

BOYLE: That's right . . .

Q: Did you visit any of the rooms of the prisoners [*sic*]?

BOYLE: No.

Boyle settled down for the night in room 621. He waffled when asked about his state of alertness. "Did you remain awake?" Silver inquired. "As far as I know, yes," Boyle answered. "Well, I'm asking you," Silver insisted. "Were you awake during that entire period?" Again Boyle wavered: "I'm pretty sure I was awake. I may have gotten groggy and dozed a little."

John Moran was the next to fess up:

Q: What time did you go to sleep on the 11th or the 12th?
MORAN: About half past one on the 12th.
Q: Where did you sleep?
MORAN: I slept in room 627 with Patrolman McLaughlin.
Q: Where were the other guards assigned that night?
MORAN: That I don't know.
Q: Before you went to the room at 1:30, when was the last time you saw Reles—how soon before?
MORAN: About fifteen or twenty minutes.
Q: Where did you see him?
MORAN: Relaxing on his bed.
Q: Was he clothed at the time?
MORAN: Yes.
Q: When was the next time you saw him?
MORAN: When he was on the roof, dead.

Moran confirmed that the guards conspired to cover up their negligence by claiming that "we walked the hall and looked in the rooms to see that the witnesses were safe":

Q: Did you all take part in the conversation?
MORAN: Yes, we all took part.
Q: Was anybody directing it?
MORAN: No.
Q: Did you all agree?
MORAN: Yes.
Q: It came voluntarily from all of you?
MORAN: Yes.

Even the once recalcitrant Victor Robbins folded. Ten years earlier, he'd taken credit for finding Reles missing during a bed check and for spotting his corpse on the extension roof. Now that the cover-up had collapsed, Robbins recalled things quite differently:

Q: When for the first time did you learn that Abe wasn't in his room?

ROBBINS: I got a call from Mr. Fulton. He said someone was out on the roof.

Q: Did you know the man [William Nicholson] from the Draft Board?

ROBBINS: I was told later on he was the one who discovered · [the body].

Yet Robbins couldn't bring himself to be completely honest. Bullheaded to the end, he hemmed and hawed when the questioning got tough:

Q: When you looked in [to room 623], did you see Reles there?

ROBBINS: I couldn't swear it was Reles. There was a person in the bed.

Q: When was the last time you peeked into the room that morning?

ROBBINS: Maybe 4:00 or 4:30.

Q: What were you doing from 4:30 until the time you learned that Abe Reles was on the roof.

ROBBINS: I don't know.

■■■

Why did the guards finally abandon the cover story that had served them so well? The short answer, as far as Ed Silver could tell, was fear. The guards knew that they would be confronted with McLaughlin's confession when they appeared before the grand jury. If they stuck to the party line, they risked being charged with perjury. And unlike their police disciplinary trial in 1941, they wouldn't have a guardian angel like Bill O'Dwyer to smooth things over for them.

Did Captain Bals know all along about the cover-up? Were his remarks to Senator Tobey about the guards falling asleep at the same time a revealing slip of the tongue rather than an off-the-wall remark? Bals bristled when Silver asked about the remark: "As far as the falling asleep question, you can't construe that literally," he snapped. "I will say now that I meant they weren't on their toes."

> Q: You were just using a figure of speech, not literally that they were actually asleep?
> BALS: That's right. How could I know what the men were doing when I was home in bed, asleep?
> Q: They could have told you.
> BALS: Nobody has ever told me anything like that.

"At no time did I know any of them were lying," Bals said, his temperature rising. "If you try to get in the record that these men told a story, and that I had any part in concocting that story, I will say it is entirely untrue." Bals needn't have gotten so hot under the collar. None of the guards ever implicated him in the cover-up.

■■■

Even after a string of setbacks—the dead-end tips and useless mystery witnesses, the meaningless testing of the makeshift rope, the scheming of Rose Reles—Silver still had something to show for the time and treasure he'd spent. After stumbling on the fact that the police guards had conspired to create a fake story and then lied their way through the disciplinary hearing, he'd adroitly turned the situation to his advantage, forcing all the cops to confess that they'd intentionally ignored orders to check on Reles during the overnight hours; that they were asleep when he went out the window; and that they'd covered up their gross negligence for ten years. Silver had cracked the case wide open. Now the question was: What would be his next move?

It was now September 1951. After five months of questioning witnesses and pursuing leads, Ed Silver was under pressure to wrap up his investigation and present his findings to the grand jury. Some of the pressure was coming from Judge Samuel Leibowitz, who was handling the legal arcana of the probe. Several times during the previous months, Silver had asked Leibowitz to extend the grand jury's term of service because he wasn't ready to make his case to them. Leibowitz had complied, but he'd warned Silver that the panel was getting impatient with the delays. Silver's boss, DA Miles McDonald, was also doing some arm twisting. He wanted the jurors to get the case before the end of the year. Silver calculated that in order to meet McDonald's fast-approaching deadline, he'd have to wrap things up as soon as possible.

The courthouse was abuzz with rumors about what Silver was planning to report to the grand jury. The press hounded him for a detailed statement, but he wasn't forthcoming: "I think we have uncovered facts that could have been uncovered at the time of Reles' death, but weren't," was all that he would say.

On September 25, Silver began presenting his findings to the grand jurors. Nine witnesses testified that first day, including William Nicholson, the draft board clerk who'd discovered Reles's body. Over the next three months, 86 witnesses testified (they were chosen by Silver out of the 150 or so he'd deposed). The parade of familiar faces included the five guards who were on duty when Reles died; Frank Bals; Elwood Divver; Detectives Charles Celano and William Cush; Edward Heffernan, James Moran, and several other former members of O'Dwyer's staff; employees and guests of the Half Moon who were at the hotel in November 1941; and a number of NYPD brass. Reles's former suite mates—Albert Tannenbaum, Sholem Bernstein, and Mickey Sycoff—also testified, though for security reasons they were questioned at a secret location with only Silver and a select group of jurors present. It didn't take a seer to predict what the three snitches would do: They put on their best poker faces, volunteered nothing, then slunk back into hiding without contributing anything new to the investigation.

There were no dramatic surprises—no "Perry Mason moments"—in the grand jury room; witnesses essentially repeated the testimony they'd given to Silver in their depositions. Rose Reles again evaded questions about the last time she saw her husband. And once again, Silver got fed up with her antics: "If you persist [in being nonresponsive] I can do nothing but join with the grand jury to cite you for contempt. Do not try the patience of these people." The reprimand, however, did not bring her around. Despite repeated threats to charge Rose with contempt, no action was taken against her. She stonewalled the investigation at every turn and got away with it.

Captain Bals used his grand jury appearance as a soapbox to proclaim his moral indignation at the guards for sleeping on the job: "I think that is the lowest thing any man can do on an important assignment," he said disgustedly. "When you assign plenty of men, that at least one of them didn't keep on his toes." (These were the same men whose praises he'd sung in 1941.) Unrepentant to the end, however, the captain refused to accept any responsibility for the death of Abe Reles.

On the plus side, several intriguing new facts came to light during the grand jury phase. Harvey McLaughlin told the jurors that while chatting about the case with another former guard (something the witnesses had been warned not to do), he learned of at least one instance of evidence tampering in the Reles case:

Q: When you fellows discovered Abie was out on the roof, did you or anybody else do anything to change the condition of Abie's room in any way to fit in with some story?

McLaughlin: No sir.

Q: Did you ever hear that anybody else did?

McLaughlin: I heard, yes, sir.

Q: That somebody had done something in the room?

McLaughlin: I heard somebody had removed something from the room.

Q: Removed what?

McLaughlin: A bottle of liquor.

Q: When did you hear that?

McLaughlin: John Moran told me the other day, when he came out of here.

Q: Was that the first time you heard it?

McLaughlin: I knew a bottle of liquor had been disposed of, but I didn't know until the other day that John had actually found it. He said he found it in the bathroom of Reles's room and dumped it out and threw it down the incinerator.

The mystery of why the crime scene photos of Reles's room didn't show any liquor or drinking paraphernalia—even though Reles had consumed a small amount of liquor shortly before he died—was finally solved. One of the guards had made it disappear as part of the cover-up.

By far the most significant new information came from Dr. Thomas Gonzales, chief medical examiner of New York City, who offered some fascinating insights into the medical evidence. For starters, Gonzales was able to rule out a lingering rumor about Reles's physical condition before he went out the window:

Q: If before he fell or went out the window, somebody were to hit him on the head with a blunt instrument—with a bat or a blackjack—or across the back with a baseball bat, that still would appear in the autopsy, wouldn't it?

Gonzales: Yes, if there were marks or bruises on the head—but there weren't. There was a little hemorrhage in the temporal muscle of the left side of the head, but no injury to the skin. There were no marks on the back indicating a blow by a baseball bat or anything like that.

Q: What then is your opinion as to whether any physical violence was effected on the body of Reles before he died?

Gonzales: I think that we reasonably can exclude physical violence before the fall, considering this autopsy record.

Gonzales was less certain, however, about the trajectory of Reles's fall:

> Q: Doctor, would you care to offer an opinion as to how the body may have landed on the roof?
>
> GONZALES: You mean how it struck the ground?
>
> Q: Exactly.
>
> GONZALES: That's a difficult thing to say. He must have struck on his feet and then went over and struck on the left side of his head, or he might have struck on the left side of the body. I wouldn't want to venture to give an opinion just how he struck when he hit the roof.
>
> Q: [If] he happens to land standing up, just plummeted down straight, wouldn't you find some fracture of his ankles or his instep or something like that?
>
> GONZALES: You might or might not. The force may be transmitted to the hip bones, into the pelvis, and cause a fracture of the spine; or he might have struck in an angled manner.

The doctor then made a mind-boggling assertion: The internal hemorrhaging described in the autopsy report suggested that Reles was *not* killed on impact. Gonzales's opinion seemed to confound Silver:

> Q: You say he wasn't dead even after he hit the roof?
>
> GONZALES: Right. He may have lived—he probably lived—several minutes or maybe a half hour . . . he didn't die instantly.
>
> Q: From the autopsy record, could you express an opinion whether it would have been possible for Reles to change his position from the place he originally fell, by creeping or crawling?
>
> GONZALES: Absolutely.
>
> Q: It's completely within the realm of possibility that with Reles's injury he might have crept in one direction or another?
>
> GONZALES: Yes.

Later, when Silver was about to finish his questioning of Gonzales, the doctor began to speculate about whether Reles fell or was pushed out of the window:

Q: Is there anything else you would like to tell us?

GONZALES: Cases of falls from heights are the most difficult to determine whether the deceased jumped or fell or if they were pushed out of a window. We have difficulty with those cases all the time. *A person may be pushed out the window without a mark being made by the assailant.*

In fact, Gonzales continued, the eighteen-inch tear found in Reles's trousers might indicate that "a fellow up in the room could have gotten hold of his pants and thrown him out the window." This was explosive stuff: an expert witness suggesting that Reles could have been murdered! But almost immediately, Gonzales seemed to realize that he had gone too far: "That is, on the other hand, of course, I don't know," the doctor fumbled. Silver didn't react like someone eager to explore the direction Gonzales had been heading. "You weren't there, that's what you mean?" he asked the doctor. "Of course, I wasn't there," replied a chastened Gonzales. "I don't know what happened." Shortly thereafter, Silver dismissed the doctor from the stand.

■■■

After the final witnesses testified in late November, the jurors deliberated in several closed sessions. At their final meeting on December 18, 1951, the panel voted. Publicly, rumors swirled that there would be no murder indictments—but no one could nail down the reason why. Were the culprits dead? Was the evidence insufficient to indict? After the vote, Silver and a handful of jurors began writing the final report. With the holidays upcoming, most observers didn't expect it to be ready until sometime in the new year. They were shocked when the ten-page report was released on December 21—just three days after the grand jury's final session.

Overall, the report reads like a rush job, with several sloppy errors regarding basic facts. For example, Reles was thirty-five when he died, not thirty-seven, as the report states; and the Half Moon Hotel was situated between *West* 28th and 29th streets, not *East* as the report has it. The report contained no supporting illustrations, documents, or notes; no sources were cited for even its most crucial findings. Although quoting grand jury testimony is illegal, the testimony could have been paraphrased, and the sources of particularly vital facts could have been identified by euphemisms such as "one of Reles's guards," "a detective assigned to the case," and so forth.

The report began by scolding the Kefauver Committee, the Senate panel that had held public hearings on organized crime in March 1951. According to the grand jury, the committee had made Reles's death "more of a riddle than ever" by focusing national attention on the case, then failing to investigate it thoroughly. As a result, the jurors decided to take on the "onerous task" of reopening the case because of their firm belief that "It is not a healthy condition for a community to be left guessing about an event that concerns the people deeply. They have a right to know all the ascertainable facts." That being said, the jurors stood firmly behind their findings: "Our report is based on credible evidence. We cannot indulge in the speculation and fancy that has been rampant for the past ten years." Finally, the panel delivered its long-awaited verdict:

> Abe Reles fell to his death as a consequence of his attempt to escape from his room, number 623, at the Half Moon Hotel between three and four o'clock on the morning of November 12, 1941.

It was a jaw-dropping and wholly anticlimactic end to a nine-month investigation. Despite a procession of witnesses whose cumulative testimony demolished the escape-attempt theory, the jurors embraced the official story. But when one searched for an explanation of *why* Reles would want to flee from his only hiding place—the all-important question of motive—the report had only this to say: "It would be sheer speculation to attempt to discern Reles's motive for wanting to escape." No explanation at all—just a flip remark and a reprehensible cop-out.

Did the jurors keep their promise to use only "credible evidence" in reaching their conclusion? Far from it. They resorted to distortions, half-truths, and flat-out lies. One of the most brazen falsehoods:

> Just beneath the window of Reles' room was a steam radiator. That morning there was found, fastened to the brass bushing connecting the top of the radiator to the steam valve, *a length of wire which extended from the bushing to the edge of the window-sill.* This wire was of the same type as that tied to the end of the bedsheets.

This was a lie. On November 12, 1941, when Detectives Celano and Cush inspected the radiator piping in Reles's room, they noticed a spot where the paint appeared to have been scraped away; this observation led to Captain McGowan's theory that the wire on the makeshift rope had been fastened there, and that it had scraped off the paint as it came undone due to Reles's weight. The grand jury knew full well, from the detectives' reports and other material, that no one at the scene of Reles's death ever saw a strip of wire still attached to the piping; nor was any such wire photographed or booked into evidence. The panel also knew that when Ed Silver questioned Celano and Cush in 1951, the two men were certain about what they'd seen ten years earlier. Celano testified first:

> Q: You saw a pipe, probably a supply pipe since you call it a valve pipe, which had a coating of paint on which you saw scrape marks?
> CELANO: Yes.
> Q: Did you see wire there?
> CELANO: No wire there.

Next, Cush backed Celano up with his testimony:

> Q: Was there anything on that pipe or radiator other than the shiny appearance of rubbing?
> CUSH: No, that's all.

Why would the jurors concoct a piece of physical evidence that didn't exist? Perhaps they felt that the escape-attempt theory seemed incomplete, that to be credible it required something more substantial than just a bit of missing paint. It needed help, and the jurors seemed willing to provide it. What made them think they could get away with referring to evidence that didn't exist? Actually, the chances of being caught were slim: Only someone who could obtain the detectives' reports or the testimony taken by Silver or the grand jury could expose the deception—and none of that material was made public after the report was released.

In dealing with the four-foot strip of wire attached to the makeshift rope, the grand jury again played fast and loose with the truth:

> The F.B.I. ascertained that this wire would not support a weight of one hundred sixty pounds. Its limit of stress was one hundred and thirty pounds. Abe Reles, who was an unusually strong and agile man, weighed between one hundred and sixty and one hundred and seventy pounds.

Here the grand jury tried to pass off the FBI's findings as conclusive. Nothing could have been further from the truth. Was the wire tied to or wound around the pipe on November 12, 1941? Since no one knew the answer, the criminalists were forced to guess when they set up the tensile strength tests. Testing based on guesswork does not yield conclusive findings, as the criminalists made clear to Silver in the disclaimers they included in each of their reports.

The description of Reles as "unusually strong and agile," implied that he would have been able to climb down the makeshift rope with ease. But Reles wasn't the picture of health the report wanted its readers to believe: His strength had been sapped by the chronic lung disease for which he'd been hospitalized just days before his death. As for his agility, that assertion was based on an anecdote about how he once installed a television aerial by climbing "a very, very high tree like a squirrel." Who supplied the anecdote? None other than that paragon of honesty, Rose Reles. Remarkable indeed that Rose remembered a fleeting incident like the installation of an aerial, but not the year she married the nimble climber who installed it.

Next, the report turned to several key parts of the escape-attempt theory:

> The latch on the window of the room below Reles's was pulled over about one quarter-inch and had to be moved before the window could be opened. A half-screen on the outside of the window was raised to within six inches from the top of the upper half of the window. This was not its usual position. On the stone window-sill of room 523, scratches were observed, as were marks of scraping on the paint of the window frame. The sole of the left shoe worn by Reles showed considerable scraping from the inner to the outer side. Such marking also appeared on the shoe on the right foot, but only at the toe.

Regarding the alleged tampering of the screen and latch, the report failed to mention that it was discovered not by the police, but by Paul Fulton, the manager of the Half Moon Hotel. As we've seen, it was Fulton who told Captain McGowan that he'd noticed "something strange" in Room 523; McGowan then used the fortuitously timed discovery to put the finishing touches on the escape-attempt theory. When Fulton testified before the grand jury, no one asked him why he'd been poking around Room 523 in the first place. Did he have an angle, a vested interest in the outcome of the case? We know that he had an unusually close relationship with the police—so close, as we have seen, that he was invited by the cops to listen to secretly taped conversations between Reles and his wife. Perhaps Fulton was some sort of police buff who was overly eager to help his pals—the cops—solve a potentially embarrassing case.

Concerning the scratch marks on the sill and window frame of Room 523 made by Reles's shoes: What scratch marks? Were these marks mentioned in the detectives' reports? No. Did a single witness testify before the grand jury about having seen the marks? Again, no. If, nevertheless, the marks did exist, was there any proof that Reles made them? Absolutely not. Was the whole thing just another effort by the jurors to bolster the escape-attempt theory? Given the panel's track record, it was certainly plausible.

The description of the scratches on Reles's shoes was remarkably detailed, given the fact that neither Silver nor the grand jury ever saw the footwear. (Once again we have to hold Captain McGowan accountable: He failed to retain the shoes as evidence.) Though the shoes were visible in the crime scene photo of Reles's body, the photo wasn't clear enough or close enough for a precise description of the scratches. The marks could have been caused by something besides contact with the windowsill of Room 523. For example, if Reles lived for a short time after his fall—as medical examiner Thomas Gonzales testified he may have—perhaps the shoes got scraped as he, in his dying moments, dragged himself along the pebble-covered extension roof.

In dealing with Reles's injuries, the grand jury tried to quash suspicions that he may have been pushed or thrown to his death. While the report noted that Reles hadn't sustained the kind of injuries to his skull, brain, or brain covering that would suggest he'd been struck on the head before his plunge, it never dealt with Dr. Gonzales's crucial testimony that a person "may be pushed out the window without a mark being made by the assailant." The panel also didn't disclose the cryptic "Withhold information by order of D.A." notation Dr. Robillard made on Reles's autopsy report.

The grand jury grew bolder with each distortion of the truth. At one point they even belittled the idea that the Mob wanted to kill Reles at all!

"There is no evidence," the report intoned, "that at any time was an attempt ever made on Reles' life while he was in police custody, either on November 12, 1941, or at any other time." Granted, no one took a shot at Reles while he was under guard. But the grand jury must have known that the Mob was gunning for him. Burton Turkus provided the panel with details of at least two plots that were narrowly averted: One called for Reles to be ambushed as he was being driven through downtown Brooklyn to the courthouse; another called for him to be cut down by hit men with high-powered rifles as he was leaving the courthouse. Former guard James Boyle told the jurors that on one occasion the guard detail was placed on high alert after it was learned that hit men from Detroit were "on a roof on Surf Avenue [across the street from the Half Moon Hotel] within rifle distance."

During the summer months, Reles and his three fellow snitches were taken on recreational outings to Heckscher Park on Long Island. The report contended that a hit man would have had ample opportunity to kill Reles during one of those outings. Since there weren't any attempts on his life at Heckscher Park, the report suggested that maybe he wasn't a marked man after all. Convoluted logic? More like deliberate deception. The jurors knew that heavily armed police officers and state troopers provided extra security on these outings. Murdering Reles at Heckscher Park, then, would not have been the cakewalk the report claimed. And the fact that no attempt was made at Heckscher Park was not proof (as the report implied) that the Mob had decided to forgive Reles for his flagrant betrayal.

The jurors' hypocrisy was a marvel. They rejected as "sheer speculation" any effort to figure out why Reles would try to escape. But when it came to theorizing about when and where the Mob might try to assassinate Reles, the jurors freely indulged in sheer speculation of their own.

Continuing the theme of security, the report had nothing good to say about the management of the squealers' suite:

> None of the five police guards were placed in command of the detail. No regular routine or procedure was prescribed for the guards to follow in the performance of their duty, and the sergeant in charge of the detail made only brief inspection visits. The guards were not required to make periodic visits to the rooms where Reles and the others stayed or slept.

Contrary to the report, the guards *were* supposed to carry out periodic visits to the snitches' rooms; they simply ignored their orders to do so. Strangely, Captain Bals's order to humor the squealers is missing from the laundry list of flaws. It probably was no accident. By remaining silent about the captain's order, the jurors were able to bury such ugly facts as Reles's abuse of the guards and Sholem Bernstein's extortion scheme.

Without mentioning him by name, Captain McGowan was lambasted for his shoddy police work:

During the course of the investigation on November 12, 1941, and thereafter, no inquiry was made of any of the employees of the hotel or any of the tenants who were in the hotel during the course of the night and morning. It should also be stated that some of the physical evidence, such as Reles' shoes and clothes, were not retained. Those exhibits which were kept were not submitted for laboratory tests. We deplore the lack of proper investigation and the loose manner in which this important occurrence was investigated.

There were two crucial mysteries associated with Reles's final hours, and the grand jury failed to solve either one. Thanks to Rose Reles's subterfuge, the panel had nothing new to relate about the controversial visit with her husband on the night of November 11; the report simply repeated the stale fact that the couple "parted on very unfriendly terms." The panel also was not able to identify the caller who inquired about the status of Room 523: "Soon after Mrs. Reles's departure, *someone* in suite [*sic*] 620 telephoned the desk of the hotel and asked the night clerk whether Room 523, the one directly below Reles' room, was vacant. He was informed that it was."

Then, without a hint of outrage over the loss of the man who had brought the Mob to its knees, the report ended with a bloodless retelling of Reles's final hours:

Upon retirement of the prisoners, the police guards also settled down for the night. Three of them went to bed. The other two who were in different and separate rooms, made themselves comfortable in chairs on which they dozed during most of the night. The quiet thus established was not broken until 7:00 a.m. when the management of the hotel telephoned to advise them that one of the prisoners was no longer in the suite.

There was not a word about the guards' conspiracy—hatched on the morning of Reles's death and maintained for ten years—to cover up their catastrophic negligence.

■■■

How can this official whitewash be explained? How could Silver, the man who gathered much of the evidence that scuttled the escape-attempt theory, have gone along with the fraud? Did he and the jurors get cold feet when faced with the near certainty of foul play in Reles's death? We'll probably never know: None of the participants ever spoke publicly about how the verdict was reached, and it's highly unlikely that a paper trail of the cover-up exists. One thing is clear: Silver and the jurors shirked their duty, just as the guards who were supposed to keep Reles alive had shirked theirs.

■■■

On the morning of December 21, 1951, Silver and several members of the grand jury gathered in the chambers of Judge Samuel Leibowitz. They were there to present a copy of the report to the judge, who had overseen legal aspects of the investigation. The ceremony was supposed to be brief, little more than a photo op. But Leibowitz shocked everyone in the room by announcing that he had doubts about the grand jury's verdict: "It is possible," he remarked, "that if in the future, at any time, today or twenty years from now, evidence should be brought forth to show that Reles was murdered, the evidence will be presented to a grand jury." For Silver and the others, who went to such great lengths to put the Reles case to bed once and for all, the judge's words must have felt like a swift kick in the teeth.

In November 1951, Burton Turkus's book *Murder, Inc.: The Story of The Syndicate* was published. Written in collaboration with veteran crime reporter Sid Feder, it's an engrossing insider's account of the Murder, Inc., affair. Perhaps the most provocative section of the book deals with Abe Reles's death. Turkus comes to a far different verdict about the fatal fall than the grand jury would reach just a few weeks after the book appeared: "By any and every logical analysis, the facts simply do not add up to escape, prank, or suicide," he concludes. "That leaves but one theory—foul play." The overwhelming weight of the evidence that Ed Silver collected in 1951—and which he and the grand jury chose to ignore, distort, and suppress—proves Turkus was right: Abe Reles was murdered.

Years after *Murder, Inc.*, was published, Turkus's opinion received support from a most unusual source. In 1962, Joseph Valachi, a soldier in New York City's Genovese crime family, was doing time on a narcotics rap in the Atlanta penitentiary when a bone-chilling rumor reached him: Vito Genovese, the family boss, had put out a contract on Valachi's life after suspecting (mistakenly) that he was a rat. Soon afterward, Valachi beat to death a fellow inmate whom he wrongly suspected was about to carry out the contract. Faced with a murder charge (not to mention the still-unfulfilled contract on his life), the panicked Valachi made an offer to federal officials that they couldn't pass up: *Get me the hell out of here and I'll tell you whatever you want to know about the Mafia.* The feds agreed, earning Valachi the dubious distinction of being the first "made" member of the Mafia to break *omertá*—the infamous code of silence—and become an informer. (A "made man" is an Italian American who has been formally inducted into the Mafia; at the ritualistic membership ceremony, the inductee is warned that if he breaks the oath of silence, he and his soul will burn in hell forever.)

A short, barrel-chested man with a crew cut and gravelly voice, Valachi was the best thing to happen to law enforcement since Abe Reles. He divulged intimate details of the Mafia's power structure, revealing that mafiosi referred to their crime syndicate as "La Cosa Nostra," or "this thing of ours." While testifying before a Senate committee in 1963, he was asked about Reles's death. "I never met anybody who thought Abe went out that window because he wanted to," he responded dryly. Valachi was just repeating underworld rumors—he wasn't privy to any inside information—but the remark made headlines. It also ruffled some feathers. Ed Silver, now Brooklyn DA, angrily rejected Valachi's claim as "a big lie." He insisted that anyone who wanted the truth about the case should refer to the 1951 grand jury report.

■■■

Who killed Abe Reles? Several factors—slipshod police work, missing items of physical evidence, the death of key witnesses, among other things—have conspired to put a conclusive answer beyond this author's reach. So while it's unlikely that all the facts in this case will ever see the light of day, some educated guesses can certainly be made about how the murder may have been carried out, while also delving into the question of who may have been behind it all.

Since this book is about the Mob, let's begin with what three of history's mightiest organized crime bosses—Charles "Lucky" Luciano, Frank Costello, and Lepke Buchalter—had to say about Reles's death. These three are the only mobsters who've ever claimed to have knowledge of Reles's final moments. To a man, the trio pinned the murder of Reles on the guards in the squealers' suite—though each offered a different version of how the crime went down. Let's take a look at whether any of their scenarios holds up under scrutiny.

Luciano was the architect of the modern American Mafia. It was his idea to structure organized crime into a national syndicate run by two dozen families; from 1931 to 1936, Luciano himself headed the largest Mafia family in New York City. In *The Last Testament of Lucky Luciano* (1975), a ghostwritten book published more than ten years after his death, Luciano was quoted as saying the following about

Reles's untimely expiration: "The way I heard it, Captain Bals stood there in the room and supervised the whole thing. Reles was sleeping and one of the guards gave him a 'tap' [hit him] with the billy club and knocked him out. Then they picked him up and heaved him out the window." Supposedly, Bals and the guards received fifty thousand dollars for the job, though Luciano made no mention of who had *ordered* and paid for the murder.

There are several problems with Luciano's version. First, we know from the medical evidence that Reles was *not* struck on the head before going out the window. Second, Captain Bals was not at the Half Moon Hotel on the night in question. Third, no evidence has ever been discovered indicating that Bals or the guards profited financially from Reles's death. After quitting the police force in December 1941, Bals held a series of unremarkable jobs, including a stint as a private detective. His deputy, Elwood Divver, landed a job as a railroad detective. As for the guards, there was no evidence of a financial windfall among them, either. James Boyle and John Moran had retired from the NYPD by 1951, but both men had to work part-time jobs just to make ends meet (Boyle as a bank guard and Moran as a bank messenger). The other guards—Harvey McLaughlin, Victor Robbins, and Francesco Tempone—were still on the force in 1951; all three were beat cops earning the designated salary.

Frank Costello was a New York City mobster whose wealth of political contacts earned him the nickname Prime Minister of the Underworld. After Costello died in 1973, his lawyer, Joseph DiMona, tendered his client's version of Reles's last moments. Two guards chloroformed Reles as he lay in bed. As they were putting together the makeshift rope to fake an escape attempt, he began to regain consciousness. After a brief struggle, one of the guards dragged him to the window and heaved him out; Reles hit the extension roof headfirst and died instantly. "Above him in the framed window," DiMona wrote in his biography of Costello, "one of the cops was angry. 'You idiot,' he bellowed to his partner. 'You threw him too far! He's supposed to fall from the building, not fly!'" Like Luciano, Costello was silent about who had ordered the killing.

This scenario can be ruled out on the basis of the medical evidence alone. Reles would have suffered massive head injuries if he had struck the extension roof headfirst. But Costello's story does focus attention on one of the great mysteries of this case. How far from the hotel wall did Reles land? The distance might tell us whether he fell, was pushed, or was thrown to his death. Since Captain McGowan never bothered to measure the distance, the correct figure will never be known. (The grand jury report settled on nine feet, but it offered no explanation about how it arrived at that figure.) In the crime scene photo showing Reles's corpse in relation to the wall, the distance between the two seems totally inconsistent with a human body falling straight down. It's possible that Reles crawled a bit after hitting the roof, but with a fractured spine, ruptured liver, and abdominal hemorrhaging, just how far could he have crept in his last minutes of life?

Lepke also indicted the guards, but he contended that Reles's murder was an involuntary act—not a paid hit. This scenario comes to us via his attorney, Bert Wegman, who learned the story of Reles's last night on earth during a visit to his client on Death Row. Lepke's version went like this: One of the guards, in a rage over Reles's humiliating pranks, slugged him in the head; when he slipped to the floor like a rag doll, the guard panicked, convinced that he'd killed the prize canary. In order to cover up the crime, he and his brethren chucked Reles out the window. The makeshift rope was an afterthought, a prop meant to create the appearance of an escape attempt.

Lepke's tale doesn't stand up under scrutiny. Like Luciano's story, it calls for an injury to Reles's head that never occurred. And we know that the guards were able to control their anger toward Reles—although he tested their patience to the core—without resorting to violence. This scenario does, however, raise a disturbing question: Who had told Lepke about Reles's loutish behavior toward the guards? The details weren't made public at the time, but someone in the know apparently believed that Lepke should be privy to what went on in the squealers' suite.

If their goal was to turn the guards into fall guys, then Luciano, Costello, and Lepke failed miserably. They must have been delusional to think that their flimsy tales would stifle speculation about Mob involvement in Reles's murder.

So was Reles's death a Mob hit? Even for an outfit as resourceful as organized crime, it would have been a tall order to kill Reles *inside* the Half Moon Hotel. It would have required a hit man (or hit men) of almost superhuman cunning and stealth to slip past the cops at the hotel's entrances, gain entry to the squealers' suite, escape the notice of the guards (and the snitches who shared the suite with Reles), commit the murder, arrange the scene to look like an accident, then flee without being detected. Yes, the obstacles were daunting, but the Mob really didn't have a choice: The various plots to kill Reles, such as cutting him down as he was being driven to or from the courthouse, had all failed. Somehow, some way, Reles had to be taken out.

Realistically speaking, wouldn't the presence of the guards torpedo any scenario involving an intruder? That was the firmly held view of John J. Ryan, a high-ranking NYPD official at the time of Reles's death. Firmly held, that is, until Ed Silver got him to concede one key point:

Q: Did you ever hear anything to the effect that Reles was pushed out of the window?

RYAN: I don't believe he was pushed out.

Q: And why do you say that?

RYAN: How could anybody come up and push him out with five cops around there?

Q: In other words you are saying that with five cops there it could not happen?

RYAN: If they were doing their duty it couldn't happen.

Q: And if they were *not* doing their duty, it is possible it could happen?

RYAN: Yes, that's right.

So were the guards doing their duty? Let's begin with the two cops who were assigned to the hotel's entrances. Did they remain at their posts throughout the night in question? According to the testimony of Alfred Wolfarth and George Govans, two employees of the Half Moon

Hotel, they did not. The two employees were unwinding in the hotel's lobby at around 4:30 a.m. when they heard a loud thud coming from the building's east side—the same side as the extension roof where Reles's body was later found. Wolfarth and Govans stated that the two guards, Charles Burns and Thomas Doyle, were also lounging in the lobby at the time but made no effort to investigate the noise. Though Burns and Doyle claimed that they *were* at their posts, one wonders what motive the two hotel employees would have had to lie.

As for the guards in the squealers' suite, we know for a fact that they were *not* doing their job. While it's possible that their negligence could have enabled someone to get into the suite and get rid of Reles, wouldn't the steel door have presented an impenetrable barrier? Not necessarily. We don't know if the guards were as lax in keeping the door secured as they were in carrying out their other duties. Could the Mob have learned about laxity—just as Lepke learned about Reles's misconduct in the suite—and could that knowledge have been employed to murder Reles?

If there was a Mob plot, who was behind it? Obviously, there's no shortage of candidates. Just about any Mob boss in the country would have leapt at the chance to bump off Reles. Who had the greatest personal interest in seeing him dead? Albert Anastasia is the clear front-runner. As long as Reles stayed alive, the electric chair loomed over Anastasia for the murder of Morris Diamond; only Reles's death could remove that possibility once and for all. Anastasia had another incentive to go after Reles. Any number of Mob bosses believed that Anastasia was partly to blame for the Reles problem in the first place. After all, it was Anastasia who, in the lingo of the Mob, had "vouched" for Reles, lifting him from obscurity into the same orbit as Mob royalty— the same royalty that was now at Reles's mercy. It was up to Anastasia to make things right.

Not that Anastasia needed to be prodded into action. He loathed squealers with the same ferocity that the rest of society loathes child molesters. The fate of Arnold Schuster is an example of Anastasia's fanatical obsession with snitches. On February 18, 1952, the twenty-four-year-old Schuster was riding the subway in Brooklyn when he recognized another passenger as Willie Sutton, a notorious bank robber who was the target of a nationwide manhunt. Schuster alerted the police, who later nabbed the fugitive. Self-effacing and shy, Schuster became an overnight celebrity. He was interviewed by several local television stations. Unfortunately, Anastasia happened to see one of the broadcasts. He flew into a blind rage. "I can't stand squealers!" he bellowed. "Hit that guy!" he ordered one of his goons, Frederick Tenuto. On March 8, 1952, Schuster was gunned down in front of his home; as he lay dying, Tenuto put a bullet through each of his eyes to deface the corpse. To cover his tracks, Anastasia later had Tenuto killed, too. No one was ever charged with Schuster's murder.

It's important to keep in mind that neither Schuster nor Sutton had any connection to the Mob. As far as Anastasia was concerned, however, it didn't matter. It was the principle of the thing: Squealers of any stripe deserve to die. And if Anastasia would risk the electric chair to kill a total stranger like Schuster who didn't pose the slightest threat to him, imagine how far he might have gone to silence Reles, the underworld's worst nightmare. Imagine, too, the chilling message that whacking Reles *inside* the Half Moon Hotel—a supposedly impenetrable fortress—would send to the rank and file of the Mob: Rats aren't safe *anywhere*.

■■■

There is a final scenario to consider. In this one, the killers enjoyed tremendous advantages over the other potential assassins we've considered. This group of killers didn't need to slip past the cops at the hotel's entrances. They didn't need to surmount the obstacle posed by the steel door to the squealers' suite. They didn't need to escape the notice of the guards in the suite. Why? Because they were already *inside* the suite.

Did Reles's own suite mates—Albert Tannenbaum, Sholem Bernstein, and Mickey Sycoff—murder him?

Did they have a motive? You bet. There was an ocean of bad blood between this trio and Reles. When Reles began squealing, they became tainted as well—spoiled goods as far as the bosses of the Mob were concerned. Soon plans were afoot for a housecleaning. Terrified hoodlums like Tannenbaum, Bernstein, and Sycoff decided to save themselves by making a beeline for O'Dwyer's office. Their lives as gangsters were over. Once they lived in the fast lane; now they spent their days cooling their heels in courthouses, preparing to condemn their former friends. Gone were the deferential looks from people in the street, the tailored clothing, the bacchanalian feasts. Now they got icy stares from their onetime associates, cheap suits provided by the DA's office, and bland room-service fare at the Half Moon Hotel. Their marriages were on the rocks, their children were forced to grow up without them—all thanks to the loathsome Reles. Filled with bitterness and self-pity, they never forgave him. Their group home, the squealers' suite, was a simmering cauldron of resentment.

Were they capable of snuffing out a life? That goes without saying. Tannenbaum, with at least six murders under his belt, had been one of Lepke's ace assassins. Bernstein had been involved in several murders, including those of Joseph Rosen (1936) and Hyman Yuran (1938). And Sycoff had a hand in the hits on Joey Amberg (1935), Solomon Goldstein (1936), and Abraham Friedman (1939).

Was the murder of Reles an impulsive act? It's entirely possible. Tannenbaum, Bernstein, and Sycoff were no longer the cool customers of their halcyon days. Pent up in the squealers' suite on an emotional razor's edge, the slightest thing could have set them off. Tannenbaum did get into fierce arguments with Reles; on at least one occasion, a minor quarrel escalated into an all-out brawl that had to be broken up by the guards. The strain of confinement was aggravated by the ongoing obligation to testify against former friends. The usually levelheaded Sholem Bernstein came unglued at the approach of an important court date. "He used to go into an awful rage," former guard Harvey McLaughlin recounted. "He wouldn't talk to anybody or he would curse you out."

Violent men, consumed with rage, living cheek-to-jowl with the cause of their woes. It isn't hard to fathom how something as trivial as a disagreeable look or cross word from the despised Reles could have detonated their hair-trigger tempers and set the wheels in motion for murder. Wouldn't Reles have put up a ferocious struggle? Not neces-sarily. Remember that he had been hospitalized for nine days in early November 1941. When he returned to the suite, he was not in the kind of shape to fight off three determined killers—especially if they got the drop on him. Wouldn't the guards have heard him fighting for his life? Again, not necessarily, especially if they were dozing at the opposite end of the suite as was their habit.

Could the murder have been premeditated? That, too, is entirely possible. Reles himself was convinced that his suite mates had it in for him. He was especially worried about what Sholem Bernstein was up to. Why Bernstein? According to Elwood Divver, Reles more than once observed Bernstein "mull over things in his life." In Reles's mind, that kind of soul searching "was a sure sign that he [Bernstein] was cracking, and that he might be planning something" against Reles.

Elwood Divver testified about the day Reles's paranoia reached a fever pitch:

Q: Was there an instance when he [Reles] went to the icebox to chop some ice and couldn't find the ice pick?

Divver: Yes.

Q: Did he raise a rumpus about it?

Divver: Yes, it was a very important case in his mind. It turned out that a detective went to the icebox to chop some ice and forgot to leave the ice pick there. He [Reles] suspected that whoever took the ice pick was planning against him.

If the killing was premeditated, would the trio have had the oppor-tunity to plan it? Absolutely. They had free access to Reles's room for the nine days he was hospitalized; plenty of time to map out the mur-der plan and decide how to stage the failed escape attempt. Wouldn't the guards have noticed them conspiring? Not likely: The laxity in the suite would have allowed the killers to operate at will. And again, Reles's weakened physical state, post-hospitalization, would have made him easier to subdue when the time came for him to die.

Wouldn't the guards have turned in the killers? Tannenbaum, Bernstein, and Sycoff knew enough about human nature to surmise that the guards would fall in line with the conspiracy the instant Reles's corpse was discovered. After all, it was the guards' failure to make their rounds that left Reles a sitting duck. The guards, therefore, had nothing to gain and everything to lose by even hinting that a homicide may have been committed on their watch.

If Tannenbaum, Bernstein, and Sycoff killed Abe Reles, they did more than just commit a murder that has remained unsolved for over a half century.

They also pulled off the ultimate inside job.

Epilogue

Here is what happened to some of the key figures in the Reles case:

ALBERT ANASTASIA spent a good part of the early 1950s trying to muscle his way into the immensely lucrative Mob-controlled casino business in Havana, Cuba. The island nation was then ruled by dictator Fulgencio Batista, who had put out the welcome mat for American gangsters in return for a generous cut of the profits. But Meyer Lansky, the Mob's man in Havana, didn't take kindly to Albert's interference, and the syndicate bosses knew that Anastasia's slash-and-burn way of doing business would spoil a very good thing. On the morning of October 25, 1957, Anastasia was getting a shave in the barbershop of a Midtown Manhattan hotel. His face was swathed in a steaming towel, so he never saw or heard the two masked gunmen who pumped ten rounds into him. The murder was never solved. The barbershop is now a Starbucks coffeehouse.

FRANK BALS eventually retired to Florida, where he became involved in the real estate business with a retired commissioner of the NYPD. In 1952, he was implicated in one of the largest corruption scandals in Brooklyn's history. Mob bookie Harry Gross, who ran a twenty-million-dollar-a-year bookmaking operation, fingered Bals as one of the police officials whom he had bribed. Bals, however, was never formally charged. He died in 1954.

ESTES KEFAUVER capitalized on his national fame by penning *Crime in America* (1951), in which he described the work of his committee as "the greatest crime hunt in history"—one that "exposed the formidable scope of organized crime and political corruption in the United States." The book became a best seller. In 1956, Senator Kefauver was chosen as Adlai Stevenson's running mate on the Democratic presidential ticket, but the pair were trounced by the Republican candidates, Dwight Eisenhower and Richard Nixon. Kefauver returned to the Senate where, on August 8, 1963, he suffered a massive heart attack while addressing his colleagues; he died two days later.

WILLIAM O'DWYER resigned as ambassador to Mexico in December 1952 but remained south of the border as an investor in various business ventures. After his brother Paul opened a law office in Mexico City, O'Dwyer worked for the firm as a "rainmaker"—trading on his name to bring in business. Beginning in 1954, he made occasional visits to New York City, though it wasn't until 1960 that he returned for good. He practiced law at his brother Paul's firm in Manhattan until his death in 1964.

BENJAMIN "BUGSY" SIEGEL decided to build the first luxury hotel-casino on the Las Vegas strip. With much fanfare, he broke ground for the Flamingo resort in 1945. But trouble wasn't long in coming. Citing cost overruns, he asked his investors—a group of East Coast mobsters who had already forked over millions—for more cash. Despite this shot in the arm, the Flamingo hemorrhaged red ink from the moment it opened in 1946. Siegel begged for more time to straighten things out, but he couldn't stanch the bleeding. To make matters worse, the investors heard rumors that Bugsy had been skimming piles of their money all along. On the night of June 20, 1947, Siegel was sitting in the living room of his mistress's Beverly Hills mansion when a fusillade of rifle bullets tore through his face and chest. The murder was never solved.

EDWARD SILVER became Brooklyn DA in 1954, and served for ten years. In 1959, his organized crime division broke up a particularly insidious loan-sharking ring that charged its customers from 200 to 1,000 percent interest on loans. In one of his most famous cases, he joined the other New York City DAs in pressing obscenity charges against John Cleland's infamous eighteenth-century novel *Memoirs of a Woman of Pleasure* (better known as *Fanny Hill*) in 1963. Silver died in 1974.

CHARLES TOBEY gained national recognition from the televised Kefauver hearings. He took advantage of his fame by penning *The Return to Morality* (1952), a heavy-handed treatise of his conservative philosophy. "For many years, an unbelievable number in America have been trying to live without God," he scolded. He counseled Americans to embrace "the ideals of the Pilgrim fathers of long ago." Tobey died in 1953; his obituary in the *New York Times* noted that his "independence and sharp tongue made him one of the more colorful figures in American public life."

BURTON TURKUS returned to private practice in 1945. In 1948, he joined the New York State Board of Mediation, where he had a long and distinguished career as an arbitrator in close to one thousand management–labor disputes. For a brief period in 1952, Turkus hosted a weekly television show on ABC called *Mr. Arsenic* (a sobriquet supposedly given to him by Martin "Buggsy" Goldstein, a Murder, Inc., defendant who went to the electric chair) in which he answered questions from an off-camera voice about gangsters in the news. Turkus died in 1982.

The fate of ALBERT TANNENBAUM, SHOLEM BERNSTEIN, and MICKEY SYCOFF is unknown.

The Half Moon Hotel was razed in 1995. A home for senior citizens now stands in its place.

Notes

Note: Unless otherwise indicated, primary source materials are from the Papers of the Kings County (Brooklyn) District Attorney, Municipal Archives of the City of New York.

Prologue

xv   **Suddenly a loud thud:** Statement of Alfred Wolfarth, April 10, 1951, "Investigation of the Death of Abe Reles," p. 1; Statement of George Govans, April 3, 1951, "Investigation of the Death of Abe Reles," p. 2. Hereafter, statements will be cited by witness name and statement date.

xvi   **It's Abe Reles:** Statement of William A. Nicholson, March 28, 1951, p. 1; Statement of Alexander Lysberg, March 27, 1951, pp. 1–2.

xvi   **send radio cars and an ambulance:** Statement of Charles F. Burns, April 30, 1951, p. 2.

xvi   **"I don't know":** Statement of Alexander Lysberg, March 27, 1951, p. 2; Statement of Victor Robbins, April 18, 1951, pp. 3–4.

xvii   **He dials up Brooklyn district attorney:** Statement of Frank Bals, June 20, 1951, pp. 9–10.

xvii   **"It's a DOA":** Statement of Dr. Max Silberman, May 1, 1951, pp. 1–4.

Chapter 1: Kid Twist and the Combination

3   **"His eyes were shiny agates":** Burton Turkus and Sid Feder, *Murder, Inc.: The Story of the Syndicate* (New York: Farrar, Straus and Young, 1951), p. 51.

4   **Reles had a volcanic temper:** Testimony of James Boyle, November 8, 1951, Kings County (Brooklyn) Grand Jury, "Investigation into the Death of Abe Reles," pp. 61, 117.

5   **"He was reluctant to pay":** "Memorandum of Information Given by Seymour Magoon Re: Killing of Irving (Puggy) Feinstein," n.d., p. 10.

5   **The future menace to society:** New York City birth certificate of Abe Reles, No. 27650 [1906].

5   **"came in time to relieve":** A. F. Landesman, *Brownsville* (New York: Bloch Publishing, 1969), pp. 1–2, 51.

6   **"nasty little slum":** *Ibid.,* p. 51.

6   **"Brownsville was tougher":** Al Hirshberg and Sammy Aaronson, *As High as My Heart: The Sammy Aaronson Story* (New York: Coward-McCann, 1957), p. 24.

6   **"Brownsville was a breeding ground":** *Ibid.,* pp. 56–58.

7   **"He had a good family background":** *Ibid.,* pp. 61–62.

8   **"do what Sammy tells you":** *Ibid.,* p. 60.

9   **"If you wanted someone to help":** *Ibid.,* pp. 42–43, 50.

9   **"I should get a better spot":** Turkus and Feder, *Murder, Inc.,* p. 300.

10   **"I remember my encounter":** Lewis Valentine, *Night Stick: The Autobiography of Lewis J. Valentine* (New York: Dial Press), 1947, p. 190.

11   **"an impatient punk":** Hirshberg and Aaronson, *As High as My Heart,* p. 59.

11   **"as casually cold-blooded":** Turkus and Feder, *Murder, Inc.,* p. 8.

12   **"bury her or buy her":** *Ibid.,* pp. 212–213.

Chapter 2: Albert's Blessing

14–15   **The waterfront economy was tailor-made:** Thomas Reppetto, *American Mafia: A History of Its Rise to Power* (New York: Henry Holt & Company, 2004), p. 222.

15   **"Albert is the head guy":** Burton Turkus and Sid Feder, *Murder, Inc.: The Story of the Syndicate* (New York: Farrar, Straus and Young, 1951), p. 468.

15   **"With him it is always kill":** Peter Maas, *The Valachi Papers* (New York: Putnam, 1968), p. 206.

16   **"We are strong":** Turkus and Feder, *Murder, Inc.,* pp. 470–472.

22   **"They never rose from Brownsville flats":** *New York Post,* April 13, 1940.

23   **"Why do you allow hoodlums":** Turkus and Feder, *Murder, Inc.,* p. 122.

Chapter 3: Judge Louis

24   **"the most dangerous criminal":** Burton Turkus and Sid Feder, *Murder, Inc.: The Story of the Syndicate* (New York: Farrar, Straus and Young, 1951), p. 331.

25   **"the worst industrial racketeer in America":** *Ibid.*

27   **"Lepke began to appreciate":** *The Life and Times of Lepke Buchalter, America's Most Ruthless Labor Racketeer* (Fort Lee, N.J.: Barricade Books, 2006), p. 13.

27   **"It was during Lepke's apprenticeship":** *Ibid.*

27   **"relentlessly consolidating their positions":** Albert Fried, *The Rise and Fall of the Jewish Gangster in America* (New York: Holt, Rinehart and Winston, 1980), p. 142.

28   **"By seizing control of the trucking business":** Jenna Weissman Joselit, *Our Gang: Jewish Crime and the New York Jewish Community, 1900–1940* (Bloomington: Indiana University Press, 1983), p. 124.

29   **"There was some kind of dispute":** "Memorandum of Information Given by Abe Reles on May 29, 1941, Re: Louis Buchalter, alias Lepke."

29   **"I just obey":** Turkus and Feder, *Murder, Inc.,* p. 332.

29   **"We did favors for them":** Joselit, *Our Gang,* p. 154.

30   **"You don't get paid for that":** Joseph Freeman, "Murder Monopoly: The Inside Story of a Crime Trust," *Nation,* May 25, 1940, p. 647.

31   **"One of the most vicious characters":** *New York Times,* October 6, 1934.

33   **"That son of a bitch Rosen":** Rich Cohen, *Tough Jews: Fathers, Sons, and Gangster Dreams* (New York: Simon & Schuster, 1998), p. 176.

33   **"That is where somebody":** "Statement of Angelo Catalano of March 25, 1940," pp. 23–29.

34   **"The bum ain't dead yet":** Fried, *Rise and Fall,* p. 206.

35   **"With this bum, you gotta":** Turkus and Feder, *Murder, Inc.,* p. 47.

Chapter 4: On the Lam

37   **"conducted midnight raids":** Robert Rockaway, *But He Was Good to His Mother: The Lives and Crimes of Jewish Gangsters* (Lynbrook, N.Y.: Gefen Books, 2000), p. 134.

37   **"bringing all the culprits to heel":** Albert Fried, *The Rise and Fall of the Jewish Gangster in America* (New York: Holt, Rinehart and Winston, 1980), p. 198.

39   **"It is apparent that the Lepke Mob":** *New York Times,* July 29, 1939.

39   **"Lepke was satisfied real good":** Burton Turkus and Sid Feder, *Murder, Inc.: The Story of the Syndicate* (New York: Farrar, Straus and Young, 1951), p. 105.

40   **"Tomorrow morning, park right here":** *Ibid.,* pp. 465–467.

40   **"received an ultimatum in a nice way":** "Memorandum of Information Given by Albert Tannenbaum Re: Lepke Hideouts," n.d., pp. 18–20.

41   **"While they ain't got you":** Turkus and Feder, *Murder, Inc.,* p. 359.

41   **Lepke's surrender:** Rich Cohen, *Tough Jews: Fathers, Sons, and Gangster Dreams* (New York: Simon & Schuster, 1998), pp. 203–208.

43   **"Albert puts the pressure on":** Stephen Fox, *Blood and Power: Organized Crime in Twentieth Century America* (New York: William Morrow, 1989), p. 217.

43–44   **Murder of Feinstein:** "Memorandum of Information Given By Abe Reles in Re: Killing of Irving Feinstein," n.d., pp. 1–8.

Chapter 5: Bill O'Dwyer's Big Gamble

45   **"Murder is safe in Brooklyn":** *New York Times,* November 1, 1938.

45–47   **The Geoghan affair:** Thomas Kessner, *Fiorello La Guardia and the Making of Modern New York* (New York: McGraw-Hill, 1989), pp. 366–367; Alan Block, *East Side, West Side: Organizing Crime in New York, 1930–1950* (New Brunswick, N.J.: Transaction Books, 1985), pp. 75–86.

47   **"vicious criminals and cheap punks":** *New York Times,* February 3, 1940.

47   **"The number of homicides not solved":** George Walsh,
       Public Enemies: The Mayor, The Mob, and the Crime That Was
       (New York: W. W. Norton, 1980), pp. 81–82.

48   **"If everybody stays on his toes":** A. F. Landesman, *Brownsville*
       (New York: Bloch Publishing, 1969), pp. 333–334.

48   **"It was a blighted area":** Burton Turkus and Sid Feder, *Murder,
       Inc.: The Story of the Syndicate* (New York: Farrar, Straus and
       Young, 1951), p. 23.

49   **"Toughs were yanked unceremoniously":** *Ibid.*, p. 28.

49   **"You've got one hell of a nerve":** *New York Times*, February 3,
       1940.

49   **"If O'Dwyer don't stop":** William O'Dwyer, *Beyond the Golden
       Door* (New York: St. John's University Press, 1987), p. 154.

49   **"I would like to talk":** "The Testimony of Harry Rudolph," n.d.

49   **"Those rats killed my friend":** *Ibid.*

50   **"This is a clean-cut charge":** *New York Times*, February 3, 1940.

50   **"We are planning to clean out":** *Ibid.*, February 4, 1940.

51   **"even the air smelled of locked doors":** Turkus and Feder,
       Murder, Inc., p. 59.

52   **"unless we got a top mobster":** *Ibid.*, pp. 49–50.

52–53 **Reles becomes a squealer:** *Ibid.*, pp. 58–64.

54   **"You don't know those bastards":** *Ibid.*, p. 443.

54   **"the most valuable deal":** *Ibid.*, p. 64.

54   **"the most effective informer":** O'Dwyer, *Golden Door*, p. 160.

54   **"Every one of those guys":** Turkus and Feder, *Murder, Inc.*,
       pp. 66–67.

55   **"He had the most amazing memory":** *Ibid.*, p. 64

55   **"a nation-wide, highly organized business":** Joseph Freeman,
       "Murder Monopoly: The Inside Story of a Crime Trust," *Nation*,
       May 25, 1940, p. 645.

56   **"rattled off names, places, facts":** Turkus and Feder, *Murder, Inc.*,
       p. 65.

56   **"For five years the possible motives":** *Ibid.*, p. 150.

58   **"Gee, I hated to take that kid":** *Ibid.*, p. 472.

58   **"I think there's six or eight":** *Ibid.*

58   **"chunks of the frozen lime":** *New York Times*, January 30, 1941.

Chapter 6: The Prize Canary

61 **"I came over to talk":** Burton Turkus and Sid Feder, *Murder, Inc.: The Story of the Syndicate* (New York: Farrar, Straus and Young, 1951), pp. 464–467.

62 **"a horror tale":** Meyer Berger, "The Strange Case of Murder, Inc.: Huge Ring Dealing in Death for Profit Is Cracked by New Brooklyn Prosecutor," *Life*, April 15, 1940, p. 97.

62 **"doing a striking job":** *New York Times*, May 13, 1940.

62 **"cutting away at the poisoned tissue":** *Ibid.*, September 20, 1940.

62 **"its most startling crime story":** Meyer Berger, "Murder, Inc.: Justice Overtakes the Largest and Most Cruel Gang of Killers in U.S. History," *Life*, September 30, 1940, p. 86.

63 **"that a man who successfully prosecuted":** Norton Mockridge and Robert H. Prall, *The Big Fix: Graft and Corruption in the World's Largest City* (New York: Henry Holt and Company, 1954), p. 55.

64 **"with the utmost ease":** *New York Times*, May 16, 1940.

65 **"You stool pigeon son of a bitch!":** Turkus and Feder, *Murder, Inc.*, p. 235.

65 **"Just tell that rat Reles":** *Ibid.*, p. 321.

66 **"I just wanted to sink my tooth":** *Ibid.*, p. 449.

66 **"These men are here":** *New York Times*, April 5, 1940.

67 **"if there is any indication":** FBI Reports No. 60–1501–41[??] * May 21, 1941, pp. 1–2, and No. 60–1501–4185, June 4, 1941.

67 **"an attempt might be made":** FBI Report No. 60–1501–4130, March 13, 1941, pp. 3–4.

68 **"O'Dwyer was informed":** FBI Report No. 60–1501–41[??] * April 2, 1941, pp. 1–2.

68 **"Reles made the statement":** FBI Report No. 60–1501–4130, March 13, 1941, p. 2.

69 **"They'll get me":** William O'Dwyer, *Beyond the Golden Door* (New York: St. John's University Press, 1987), p. 158.

---

*Due to poor reproduction of this document by the FBI, the last two digits of the report number are illegible.

70   **remodeling that would be needed:** Turkus and Feder, *Murder, Inc.,* pp. 436–437.

71–73   **Background of squealers:** NYPD rap sheets of Bernstein, Tannenbaum, and Sycoff.

74   **"Hey Burt":** Turkus and Feder, *Murder, Inc.,* p. 435.

Chapter 7: Homicide Squad

75   **"What the hell happened?":** Statement of John E. Moran, April 25, 1951, p. 12, "Investigation by Assistant District Attorney Edward Heffernan into Cause of Death of Abe Reles, November 12, 1941," p. 57. Hereafter cited as "Investigation by Heffernan."

75   **"You better get your stories straight!":** Testimony of Harvey McLaughlin, November 8, 1951, Kings County (Brooklyn) Grand Jury, "Investigation into the Death of Abe Reles," p. 21.

75   **"an unknown DOA":** Entry in 60th Precinct telephone log for November 12, 1941.

76   **Donovan was astonished:** Statement of Joseph F. Donovan, May 9, 1951, pp. 1–2.

78   **he called Assistant DA Edward Heffernan:** Statement of Edward A. Heffernan, April 24, 1951, pp. 2–3.

79   **"I opened up my door":** "Investigation by Heffernan," p. 7.

79   **"she never asked me":** *Ibid.,* p. 9.

79   **"What supervision do they have":** *Ibid.,* pp. 9, 10.

80   **"As far as your room is concerned":** *Ibid.,* p. 4.

80   **"didn't even like being":** *Ibid.,* p. 10.

80   **he suffered from bronchiectasis:** Statement of Dr. Philip Nash, April 3, 1951, pp. 1–2.

81   **"The coat is turned up":** "Investigation by Heffernan," p. 12.

82   **one photograph—and only one:** Photograph taken by Harold O'Neil, NYPD Bureau of Criminal Identification, at the scene of the death of Abe Reles.

82   **The doctor reckoned:** Statement of Frank Bals, June 21, 1951, p. 11.

82   **McGowan ordered Patrolman Paul Johnston:** Statement of Paul Johnston, April 30, 1951, pp. 1–3.

83   **Johnston found a Waltham pocket watch:** NYPD Property Clerk's Voucher No. 207, November 12, 1941.

83   **McGowan picked it up:** Photograph taken by Harold O'Neil, NYPD Bureau of Criminal Identification, at scene of death of Abe Reles.

83   **The captain ordered Detectives Cush and Celano:** Statement of Charles P. Celano, May 2, 1951, p. 6.

84   **he'd just found "something strange":** Statement of Charles P. Celano, May 2, 1951, pp. 8–9; Statement of William T. Cush, May 2, 1951, pp. 9–10.

Chapter 8: A Fatal Misstep

85   **"more of the insulated wire":** "Investigation by Heffernan," pp. 12, 33.

85   **Meanwhile, Captain Bals suddenly realized:** Statement of John H. McCarthy, April 16, 1951, p. 2; Statement of Rose Reles, March 26, 1951, pp. 4–6.

86   **"They won't tell me what's wrong":** "Investigation by Heffernan," p. 13.

86   **"Now, during the course":** *Ibid.*, p. 14.

87   **"When did you first discover":** *Ibid.*, p. 16.

87   **"You had not been notified":** *Ibid.*, p. 19.

87   **"When Detective Robbins":** *Ibid.*, p. 26.

88   **"about an hour":** *Ibid.*, p. 16.

88   **"You say you went into his room":** *Ibid.*, p.17. Emphasis added.

88   **"How frequently had you visited":** *Ibid.*, p. 30.

89   **"How frequently had you seen him":** *Ibid.*, pp. 37, 38.

89   **"Had you heard any disturbance":** *Ibid.*, p. 25.

89   **"Did he ever say or do":** *Ibid.*, p. 47.

89   **"During the time that you":** *Ibid.*, p. 33.

90   **"Was there anything that would indicate":** *Ibid.*, p. 41.

90   **"He used to look for the guard":** *Ibid.*

90   **"Now when these witnesses retire":** *Ibid.*, p. 50.

90   **"Had you ever had any indication":** *Ibid.*

91   **"How frequently did your men supervise":** *Ibid.*, p. 58.

91   **"was of the strictest":** *Ibid.*, pp. 60, 56.

91   **"Have you a theory":** *Ibid.*, pp. 53–54.

92 **"the shiny surface":** *Ibid.*, p. 58.

92 **"Was there anything in his attitude":** *Ibid.*, p. 56.

93 **"There are five guards working":** *New York Journal-American*, November 13, 1941.

94 **Heffernan walked the DA through:** Statement of Edward A. Heffernan, April 24, 1951, pp. 4–5.

94 **McGowan didn't perform any better:** Statement of Charles P. Celano, May 2, 1951, p. 7; Statement of William T. Cush, May 2, 1951, p. 12; NYPD Property Clerk's Voucher No. 207, November 12, 1941.

95 **Dr. Gregory Robillard performed the autopsy:** Abe Reles autopsy report, November 12, 1941; Statement of Charles P. Celano, May 2, 1951, p. 11.

95 **"Withhold information":** Handwritten note by Dr. Gregory Robillard on Reles's autopsy.

96 **"What have they done to him?":** Statement of Frank Bals, June 21, 1951, p. 27.

96 **"between 7:00 & 7:15 a.m.":** NYPD "Report of Unusual Occurrence by Detectives," Case No. 487, November 12, 1941.

96 **"lowered himself to the window":** NYPD Complaint Report, Case No. 487, November 12, 1941.

Chapter 9: The Law of Gravity

98 **"I haven't been able to sleep":** Burton Turkus and Sid Feder, *Murder, Inc.: The Story of the Syndicate* (New York: Farrar, Straus and Young, 1951), p. 438.

98 **"It was a great game":** Rich Cohen, *Tough Jews: Fathers, Sons, and Gangster Dreams* (New York: Simon & Schuster, 1998), p. 227.

98 **"the only law that got him":** *Newsweek*, November 24, 1941.

98 **"We were well rid of him":** Lewis Valentine, *Night Stick: The Autobiography of Lewis J. Valentine* (New York: Dial Press), 1947, p. 190.

99 **"an examination of the pipe":** NYPD "Supplementary Complaint Report," Case No. 487, November 13, 1941, pp. 1, 3.

99 **In keeping with Orthodox religious practice:** Statement of Jacob Misikoff, April 30, 1951, p. 1; *Brooklyn Eagle*, November 14, 1941; *Newsweek*, November 24, 1941.

100   **"The wails of the widow":** *Brooklyn Eagle,* November 14, 1941.

100   **"supported her as she stumbled":** *Ibid.*

100   **"Mrs. Reles's steady wail":** *Ibid.*

100   **"Damn the newspapers!":** *Ibid.*

100   **"We've lived a life of terror":** *Newsweek,* November 24, 1941.

101   **"I felt reasonably assured":** William O'Dwyer, *Beyond the Golden Door* (New York: St. John's University Press, 1987), p. 162.

101   **"Reminds me of my opponent's head":** Thomas Kessner, *Fiorello La Guardia and the Making of Modern New York* (New York: McGraw-Hill, 1989), p. 499.

101   **"I wish there was some other":** *New York Times,* November 14, 1941.

102   **"did at some time prior":** NYPD, "In the Matter of Charges Against James Boyle, et al.," November 26, 1941, pp. 1–3. Hereafter cited as "Charges."

103   **"I have the highest opinion":** "Charges," p. 12.

103   **"it must have been during that time":** *Ibid.,* p. 17.

103   **"while on his usual rounds":** *Ibid.,* p. 15.

103   **"a rather trying assignment":** *Ibid.,* p. 21.

103   **"I would say that they carried out":** *Ibid.,* pp. 24–25.

103   **"instructed to pay particular attention":** *Ibid.,* p. 25.

104   **"were assigned to prevent harm":** *Ibid.,* p. 28.

104   **"to prevent any harm coming":** *Ibid.,* pp. 30–31.

104   **"all five of us":** *Ibid.,* p. 33.

104   **other defendants gave virtually identical testimony:** *Ibid.,* pp. 38, 41, 42, 44–45.

105   **"This report will show":** *New York Times,* December 3, 1941.

105   **the results of Reles's toxicology tests:** Office of the Chief Medical Examiner, City of New York, Chemical Report No. 2134-41, n.d.

106   **"CASE CLOSED":** NYPD "Supplementary Complaint Report," Case No. 487, December 31, 1941.

Chapter 10: A Perfect Murder Case

107   **"Even as America fought":** Rich Cohen, *Tough Jews: Fathers, Sons, and Gangster Dreams* (New York: Simon & Schuster, 1998), p. 231.

108   **"The corroboration supplied by Reles":** Burton Turkus,

"Confidential Memorandum Re: Anastasia," April 8, 1942.

108   **O'Dwyer decided to drop his pursuit:** Burton Turkus and Sid
Feder, *Murder, Inc.: The Story of the Syndicate* (New York: Farrar,
Straus and Young, 1951), pp. 480–481.

108   **"as close to O'Dwyer as his shirt":** George Walsh, *Public Enemies:
The Mayor, The Mob, and the Crime That Was* (New York: W. W.
Norton, 1980), p. 209.

109   **"If [gangsters] are here":** *New York Times,* October 31, 1945.

110   **We find that every case:** Quoted in US Senate, Special Committee
to Investigate Organized Crime in Interstate Commerce, The
Kefauver Committee Report on Organized Crime (New York, 1951),
p. 108. Hereafter cited as Kefauver Committee Report.

110   **"As long as Abe Reles was alive":** Speech by William O'Dwyer,
WNYC Radio, October 30, 1945, reprinted in *New York Times,*
October 31, 1945.

111   **"Well, Mr. O'Dwyer":** Speech by George J. Beldock Jr., WMCA
Radio, October 31, 1945, reprinted in *New York Times,* November 1,
1945.

112   **"a witch hunt":** Alan Block, *East Side, West Side: Organizing Crime
in New York, 1930–1950* (New Brunswick, N.J.: Transaction Books,
1985), p. 119.

112   **the White House made a startling:** Norton Mockridge and Robert
H. Prall, *The Big Fix: Graft and Corruption in the World's Largest
City* (New York: Henry Holt and Company, 1954), p. 235.

113   **"Halley came to see me":** William O'Dwyer, *Beyond the Golden
Door* (New York: St. John's University Press, 1987), p. 360.

113   **"Businesses were paralyzed":** Estes Kefauver, *Crime in America*
(New York: Doubleday, 1951), p. 283.

114   **Testimony of Frank Bals:** Reprinted in *New York Times,*
March 16, 1951.

114   **"The day I left for Mexico":** O'Dwyer, *Golden Door,* pp. 362–363.

115   **"There was noise and confusion":** *Ibid.,* p. 363.

115   **"in excellent physical condition":** *New York Times,* March 20, 1951.

115-117 **Testimony of William O'Dwyer:** Reprinted in *ibid.,* March 20, 21,
1951.

117   **"Asked what he did to establish responsibility":** Kefauver

ommittee Report, pp. 109–110.

"Neither O'Dwyer nor his appointees": *Ibid.,* p. 225. Emphasis
added.

117 **"You don't kill public men today":** *Collier's,* August 21, 1953.

118 **"The Man Who Won't Come Home":** *Ibid.,* August 7, 1953.

Chapter 11: Hot Tips and Mystery Witnesses

121 **"I am thankful":** *New York Times,* March 20, 1951.

123 **"That photograph wouldn't show":** Excerpt from testimony of
Frank Bals, reprinted in *New York Times,* March 16, 1951.

123 **Silver briefly considered exhuming:** Edward Silver memorandum
of telephone conversation with Dr. Thomas Gonzales, May 14, 1951.

123 **"I saw a body falling":** Statement of Lessie Gold, December 10,
1951.

124 **"They bagged him":** Anthony Corpolongo to Miles McDonald,
June 24, 1951; Memorandum from Assistant DAs Lewis Joseph
and Kenneth McCabe to Edward Silver, July 10, 1951.

124 **"I wonder whether the officers":** Elbrige Gatewood to Edward
Silver, September 26, 1951.

125 **"the third degree":** "A Loyal Citizen" to DA Miles McDonald, n.d.

125 **"Now listen to this":** Anonymous to Edward Silver, n.d.

125 **"She appeared to be very much disturbed":** Memorandum from
Assistant DA Morgan Lane to Edward Silver, March 27, 1951.

125 **"some new and very interesting information":** *New York Times,*
March 26, 1951.

125 **"I don't know whether they were used":** *New York Times,* March
28, 1951.

126 **"A sensational break is expected soon":** Edward Silver
memorandum of telephone conversation with Rose Bigman
(Winchell's secretary), June 12, 1951.

126 **"DID ABE RELES FALL":** New York *Daily News,* April 8, 1951.

126 **"Questions Kefauver Didn't Ask":** *People Today,* April 25, 1951,
p. 7.

127 **"he would never play a joke":** New York *Daily News,* March 26, 1951.

127 **"Search of the records":** Memorandum from Lieutenant Howard

Finney, NYPD, to Edward Silver, May 8, 1951.

127 **"considerable redecoration":** U.S. Navy, "Supplement to the Fourth Quarterly Sanitary Report," June 15, 1946.

129 **"Statements made by me":** Senator Charles Tobey to Edward Silver, December 5, 1951.

130 **"Reles Death Jury to Hear O'Dwyer":** *New York Times,* November 30, 1951.

130 **"a further course of action":** *New York Times,* December 9, 1951.

130 **"I have received your telegram":** William O'Dwyer to Edward Silver, December 10, 1951.

131 **"political attack":** *New York Times,* March 26, 1951.

Chapter 12: To Flee or Not to Flee

132 **"Anywhere in the world":** Burton Turkus and Sid Feder, *Murder, Inc.: The Story of the Syndicate* (New York: Farrar, Straus and Young, 1951), p. 443.

132 **"From your talks with Reles":** Statement of Elwood J. Divver, May 1, 1951, pp. 4–5.

133 **"He was in fear that the Mob":** *Ibid.,* p. 5.

134 **Fearful of being poisoned:** *Ibid.,* p. 9.

134 **"From your observations of him":** Statement of Frank Bals, June 20, 1951, p. 21.

134 **"His demeanor and conduct with me":** *Ibid.,* p. 19.

134 **"What you are trying to tell me":** *Ibid.,* p. 20.

135 **"He always said":** Statement of Victor Robbins, April 18, 1951, p. 8.

135 **"He would want you to sit":** Statement of Harvey McLaughlin, April 5, 1951, p. 27.

135 **He found that Reles's family:** Statement of George Bopp, May 8, 1951, p. 1; Statement of Thomas Dolan, May 8, 1951, p. 1; Statement of Martin Rafferty, May 8, 1951, p. 1.

136 **"Reles was looking forward":** Turkus and Feder, *Murder, Inc.,* p. 444.

136 **"As far as the escape theory,"** Edward Silver memorandum of telephone conversation with Hyman Barshay, July 18, 1951.

136 **"allowed to save his life":** *New York Times,* September 20, 1940.

137 **"Was there any information":** Statement of Joseph F. Donovan,

May 9, 1951, pp. 7–8.

137 **"seemed to have an optimistic view":** Statement of Elwood Divver, May 1, 1951, pp. 6–7.

137 **"How long before he died":** Statement of Frank Bals, June 20, 1951, pp. 40, 41.

137-138 **Reles gave O'Dwyer information linking Joe Adonis:** Turkus and Feder, *Murder, Inc.*, pp. 451–452.

138 **"For months I tried":** Norton Mockridge and Robert H. Prall, *The Big Fix: Graft and Corruption in the World's Largest City* (New York: Henry Holt and Company, 1954), p. 59.

138 **"I charge that O'Dwyer has failed":** *Ibid.*, p. 277.

138 **"the strain was too much":** Meyer Berger, "Lepke: The Shy Boss of Bloody Murder, Inc. Awaits Death in the Electric Chair," *Life*, February 28, 1944, p. 95.

139 **anecdotal evidence that he wasn't suicidal:** "Investigation by Heffernan," pp. 19, 23, 47.

139 **"was in a very good mood":** Statement of George Govans, April 3, 1951, pp. 1–2.

139 **"I don't think Abe was that type":** Statement of Harvey McLaughlin, April 5, 1951, p. 27.

140 **"Isn't it true that":** Statement of Frank Bals, June 20, 1951, pp. 21, 22; Statement of Frank Bals, June 21, 1951, p. 34.

140 **"asking if there was anybody":** Statement of Alexander Lysberg, March 27, 1951, p. 1.

142 **Silver received the test results:** FBI Lab Report No. PC-30159GR, May 12, 1951.

142 **"a number of new problems":** Edward Silver to Messrs. Donaldson and Harbo, FBI Laboratory, June 27, 1951.

143 **On July 9, the FBI reported:** FBI Lab Report No. PC-30537GR, July 9, 1951.

143 **Hoover had to send him a letter:** J. Edgar Hoover to Edward Silver, July 26, 1951.

143 **"The Reles stamp was not there":** Turkus and Feder, *Murder, Inc.*, p. 445.

Chapter 13: The Widow's Revenge

145   **"disdain, contempt and scorn":** *New York Times,* June 5, 1942.

145   **"I would answer":** Statement of Rose Reles, March 26, 1951, p. 12.

145   **"When did you marry Reles?":** *Ibid.,* p. 1.

146   **"How did you think he was":** Statement of Rose Reles, April 26, 1951, pp. 14–16.

147   **"He would buy up every single paper":** *Ibid.,* p. 41.

147   **"How long did you spend with Reles":** Statement of Rose Reles, March 26, 1951, p. 3.

147   **"You were there almost three hours":** Statement of Rose Reles, March 28, 1951, p. 1.

147   **"I didn't talk":** Statement of Rose Reles, March 26, 1951, pp. 3, 23.

148   **"the true reason":** Statement of Rose Reles, April 26, 1951, pp. 5, 6, 9.

148   **"Is there anything that you can tell me":** Statement of Rose Reles, March 26, 1951, pp. 18–19.

149   **"You don't know that Abe got out":** Statement of Rose Reles, April 26, 1951, p. 36.

150   **"He tied a sheet":** *Ibid.,* p. 34. Emphasis added.

150   **"I think I am the only one":** *Ibid.,* p. 36.

150   **"Did you question her":** Statement of Frank Bals, June 21, 1951, p. 27.

151   **"in order to check up on":** Statement of Elwood J. Divver, May 1, 1951, pp. 21–22.

151   **the searches proved fruitless:** Memorandum from Assistant DA Lewis Joseph to Edward Silver, July 9, 1951.

151   **"If I told you":** Statement of Frank Bals, June 21, 1951, p. 25.

Chapter 14: Tin Badge Cops

153   **"a lot of humoring":** "Investigation by Heffernan," p. 59.

153   **"Our job was to humor them":** *Ibid.,* p. 34.

153   **"Keep them happy":** Statement of Victor Robbins, April 18, 1951, p. 2.

153   **"under a strain":** Statement of Harvey McLaughlin, April 5, 1951, p. 8.

153   **Most of the humoring, Silver found:** *Ibid.,* p. 23.

154   **"You wrote that":** Burton Turkus and Sid Feder, *Murder, Inc.: The Story of the Syndicate* (New York: Farrar, Straus and Young, 1951), p. 451.

154   **"Why don't you get wise?":** Sholem Bernstein to "Whitey," n.d.

154   **"Now I'm raising it":** *Ibid.*

155   **Winchell immediately printed excerpts:** *New York Daily Mirror,* April 3, 1951.

155   **"Abe was very abusive":** Statement of Harvey McLaughlin, April 5, 1951, p. 6.

155-156   **"We are making a check":** Turkus and Feder, *Murder, Inc.,* p. 447.

156   **"What are you guys going to get":** Testimony of Harvey McLaughlin, November 8, 1951, Kings County (Brooklyn) Grand Jury, "Investigation into the Death of Abe Reles," p. 7.

156   **"That's what you're getting paid for":** Testimony of James Boyle, November 8, 1951, Kings County (Brooklyn) Grand Jury, "Investigation into the Death of Abe Reles," p. 70.

156   **"I don't know anybody":** Statement of Harvey McLaughlin, April 5, 1951, pp. 5, 8.

157   **"Did you have a regular routine":** *Ibid.,* p. 9. Emphasis added.

157   **"Did you see them up":** *Ibid.,* p. 25.

158   **"Prior to learning":** Statement of Francesco Tempone, April 18, 1951, pp. 2, 3.

158   **"After Detective Robbins":** *Ibid.,* pp. 6–7.

159   **"I moped around":** Statement of James Boyle, April 18, 1951, pp. 4, 6.

160   **"Did you remain awake?":** *Ibid.,* p. 6.

160   **"What time did you go to sleep":** Statement of John E. Moran, April 25, 1951, p. 2.

160   **"we walked the hall":** *Ibid.,* p. 6.

161   **"When for the first time":** Statement of Victor Robbins, April 18, 1951, pp. 3, 4.

161   **"When you looked in":** *Ibid.,* pp. 2, 3.

162   **"As far as the falling asleep question":** Statement of Frank Bals, June 20, 1951, p. 15.

162   **"At no time":** Statement of Frank Bals, June 21, 1951, p. 16.

Chapter 15: Verdict

163   **"I think we have uncovered facts":** *New York Times*, September 23, 1951.

163   **Silver began presenting his findings:** *Ibid.*, September 26, 1951; Memorandum for the record, "Witnesses Interviewed But Not Used," p. 1, n.d.

164   **"If you persist":** Testimony of Rose Reles, November 19, 1951, Kings County (Brooklyn) Grand Jury "Investigation into the Cause of Death of Abraham Reles," p. 7. Hereafter, grand jury testimony will be cited by witness's name and date of testimony.

164   **"I think that is the lowest thing":** Testimony of Frank Bals, November 19, 1951, p. 43.

164   **"When you fellows discovered":** Testimony of Harvey McLaughlin, November 8, 1951, pp. 25–26.

165   **"If before he fell":** Testimony of Dr. Thomas Gonzales, November 1, 1951, p. 28.

166   **"Doctor, would you care to offer":** *Ibid.*, pp. 34, 35.

166   **"You say he wasn't dead":** *Ibid.*, pp. 26, 28–29.

167   **"Is there anything else":** *Ibid.*, pp. 32, 37–38. Emphasis added.

168   **"more of a riddle than ever":** Kings County Grand Jury Presentment, "Investigation into the Cause of Death of Abe Reles," December 21, 1951, p. 1. Hereafter cited as "Presentment."

168   **"Abe Reles fell to his death":** "Presentment," p. 2.

168   **"It would be sheer speculation":** *Ibid.*, p. 10.

169   **"Just beneath the window":** *Ibid.*, pp. 2–3. Emphasis added.

169   **"You saw a pipe":** Statement of Charles P. Celano, May 2, 1951, p. 6.

169   **"Was there anything":** Statement of William T. Cush, May 2, 1951, p. 6.

170   **"The F.B.I. ascertained":** "Presentment," p. 3.

170   **"unusually strong":** Testimony of Rose Reles, November 19, 1951, pp. 46–47.

171   **"The latch on the window":** "Presentment," pp. 8, 7.

172   **"There is no evidence":** *Ibid.*, p. 6.

172   **"on a roof on Surf Avenue":** Testimony of James Boyle, November 8, 1951, p. 74.

173 **"None of the five":** "Presentment," p. 6.

174 **"During the course of the investigation":** *Ibid.,* p. 9.

174 **"parted on very unfriendly terms":** *Ibid.,* p. 8.

174 **"Soon after Mrs. Reles's departure":** *Ibid.* Emphasis added.

174 **"Upon retirement of the prisoners":** *Ibid.*

175 **"It is possible":** *New York Times,* December 22, 1951.

Chapter 16: Musings on Murder

176 **"By any and every logical analysis":** Burton Turkus and Sid Feder, *Murder, Inc.: The Story of the Syndicate* (New York: Farrar, Straus and Young, 1951), p. 449.

177 **"I never met anybody":** Peter Maas, *The Valachi Papers* (New York: Putnam, 1968), p. 176.

177 **"a big lie":** *New York Times,* October 2, 1963.

178 **"The way I heard it":** Martin A. Gosch and Richard Hammer, *The Last Testament of Lucky Luciano* (Boston: Little, Brown, 1975), p. 253.

178 **no evidence . . . that Bals or the guards profited financially:** Statement of Frank Bals, June 20, 1951, p. 2; Statement of Elwood Divver, May 1, 1951, pp. 22, 23. See the first page of the statements of the five guards for their financial information.

178 **"Above him in the framed window":** George Wolf and Joseph DiMona, *Frank Costello: Prime Minister of the Underworld* (New York: William Morrow, 1974), pp. 124–125.

179 **Lepke's version went like this:** Edward Silver memorandum of telephone conversation with Bert Wegman, July 12, 1951.

180 **"Did you ever hear":** Statement of John J. Ryan, May 2, 1951, p. 7. Emphasis added.

182 **"I can't stand squealers!":** Maas, *Valachi Papers,* p. 206.

183 **"He used to go into an awful rage":** Statement of Harvey McLaughlin, April 5, 1951, p. 11.

184 **"mull over things":** Statement of Elwood J. Divver, May 1, 1951, p. 15.

184 **"Was there an instance":** *Ibid.*

Bibliography

Manuscript Collection
Papers of the Kings County (Brooklyn) District Attorney, Municipal Archives
of the City of New York.

Books
Asbury, Herbert. *Gangs of New York.* New York: Alfred A. Knopf, 1928.

Block, Alan. *East Side, West Side: Organizing Crime in New York, 1930–1950.* New Brunswick, N.J.: Transaction Books, 1985.

Cohen, Rich. *Tough Jews: Fathers, Sons, and Gangster Dreams.* New York: Simon & Schuster, 1998.

Collins, Frederick L. *Homicide Squad.* New York: G. P. Putnam's Sons, 1944.

Dewey, Thomas E. *Twenty Against the Underworld.* New York: Doubleday, 1974.

Downey, Patrick. *Gangster City: The History of the New York Underworld, 1900–1935.* Fort Lee, N.J.: Barricade Books, 2004.

Fox, Stephen. *Blood and Power: Organized Crime in Twentieth Century America.* New York: William Morrow, 1989.

Fried, Albert. *The Rise and Fall of the Jewish Gangster in America.* New York: Holt, Rinehart and Winston, 1980.

Gabler, Neal. *Winchell: Gossip, Power and the Culture of Celebrity.* New York: Alfred A. Knopf, 1994.

Gosch, Martin A., and Richard Hammer. *The Last Testament of Lucky Luciano.* Boston: Little, Brown, 1975.

Hirshberg, Al, and Sammy Aaronson. *As High as My Heart: The Sammy Aaronson Story.* New York: Coward-McCann, 1957.

Howe, Irving. *World of Our Fathers.* New York: Bantam, 1980.

Immerso, Michael. *Coney Island: The People's Playground.* New Brunswick, N.J.: Rutgers University Press, 2002.

Jackson, Kenneth T., and John B. Manbock. *The Neighborhoods of Brooklyn.* New Haven, Conn.: Yale University Press, 1998.

Jennings, Dean. *We Only Kill Each Other: The Life and Bad Times of Bugsy Siegel.* Englewood Cliffs, N.J.: Prentice Hall, Inc., 1968.

Joselit, Jenna Weissman. *Our Gang: Jewish Crime and the New York Jewish Community, 1900–1940.* Bloomington: Indiana University Press, 1983.

Katz, Leonard. *Uncle Frank: The Biography of Frank Costello.* New York: Drake, 1973.

Kavieff, Paul F. *The Life and Times of Lepke Buchalter, America's Most Ruthless Labor Racketeer.* Fort Lee, N.J.: Barricade Books, 2006.

Kefauver, Estes. *Crime in America.* New York: Doubleday, 1951.

Kessner, Thomas. *Fiorello La Guardia and the Making of Modern New York.* New York: McGraw-Hill, 1989.

Lacey, Robert. *Little Man: Meyer Lansky and the Gangster Life.* Boston: Little, Brown, 1991.

Landesman, A. F. *Brownsville.* New York: Bloch Publishing, 1969.

Lardner, James, and Thomas Reppetto. *NYPD: A City and Its Police.* New York: Henry Holt and Company, 2000.

Limpus, Lowell M. *Honest Cop: Lewis J. Valentine.* New York: E. P. Dutton, 1939.

Maas, Peter. *The Valachi Papers.* New York: Putnam, 1968.

Mockridge, Norton, and Robert H. Prall. *The Big Fix: Graft and Corruption in the World's Largest City.* New York: Henry Holt and Company, 1954.

Moore, William Howard. *The Kefauver Committee and the Politics of Crime, 1950–1952.* Columbia: University of Missouri Press, 1974.

O'Dwyer, William. *Beyond the Golden Door.* New York: St. John's University Press, 1987.

Peterson, Virgil. *The Mob: Two Hundred Years of Organized Crime in New York.* Ottawa, Ill.: Green Hill Publishers, 1983.

Reid, Ed. *The Shame of New York.* New York: Random House, 1953.

Reppetto, Thomas. *American Mafia: A History of Its Rise to Power.* New York: Henry Holt and Company, 2004.

Rockaway, Robert. *But He Was Good to His Mother: The Lives and Crimes of Jewish Gangsters.* Lynbrook, N.Y.: Gefen Books, 2000.

Seidman, Harold. *Labor Czars: A History of Labor Racketeering.* New York: Liveright, 1938.

Smith, Richard Norton. *Thomas E. Dewey and His Times.* New York: Simon & Schuster, 1982.

Swanstrom, Edward E. *The Waterfront Labor Problem.* New York: Fordham University Press, 1938.

Thompson, Craig, and Raymond Allen. *Gang Rule in New York.* New York: Dial Press, 1947.

Turkus, Burton, and Sid Feder. *Murder, Inc.: The Story of the Syndicate.* New York: Farrar, Straus and Young, 1951.

US Senate, Special Committee to Investigate Organized Crime in Interstate Commerce. The Kefauver Committee Report on Organized Crime. Washington, D.C.: US Government Printing Office, 1951.

Valentine, Lewis J. *Night Stick: The Autobiography of Lewis J. Valentine.* New York: Dial Press, 1947.

Walsh, George. *Public Enemies: The Mayor, The Mob, and the Crime That Was.* New York: W. W. Norton, 1980.

Wolf, George, and Joseph DiMona. *Frank Costello: Prime Minister of the Underworld.* New York: William Morrow, 1974.

Articles

Berger, Meyer. "The Strange Case of Murder, Inc.: Huge Ring Dealing in Death for Profit Is Cracked by New Brooklyn Prosecutor." *Life,* April 15, 1940.

———. "Murder, Inc.: Justice Overtakes the Largest and Most Cruel Gang of Killers in U.S. History." *Life,* September 30, 1940.

———. "Lepke: The Shy Boss of Bloody Murder, Inc. Awaits Death in the Electric Chair." *Life,* February 28, 1944.

Freeman, Joseph. "Murder Monopoly: The Inside Story of a Crime Trust." *Nation,* May 25, 1940.

———. "How Murder, Inc. Trains Killers." *American Mercury,* October 1940.

Slonim, Joel. "The Jewish Gangster." *Reflex* 3, no. 1 (July 1928).

Velie, Lester. "William O'Dwyer: The Man Who Won't Come Home." *Collier's,* August 7, August 21, 1953.

Index

Acknowledgments

I've had the great good fortune of working with consummate professionals at every stage of this project.

Ed Knappman, agent extraordinaire, was an early champion of this book. He stayed the course of this venture with an expert hand on the tiller.

Philip Turner appreciated the compelling nature of Abe Reles's story, and he did me the great honor of accepting the manuscript for publication by Union Square Press. He also offered incisive suggestions on how to improve the work, as did Alan Bisbort. From there, Iris Blasi, with great aplomb, shepherded the manuscript through the labyrinthine publishing process. Laura Jorstad did an impeccable job of copyediting, Tania Bissell's proofreading was top-notch, and Andrea Santoro was a first-rate project editor. The creative talents of Chrissy Kwasnik, who designed the book, and Elizabeth Mihaltse, who created the cover, were nothing short of remarkable.

Kenneth Cobb, former director of the New York City Municipal Archives, answered my requests for information when this work was in its infancy. Michael Lorenzini, also of the Archives, Elizabeth Harvey of the Brooklyn Public Library's Brooklyn Collection, and Mark Lewis of the Library of Congress all provided expert assistance. Alan Bisbort's early critique of the manuscript was insightful. Vicki Harlow was a constant source of enthusiasm.

Many moons ago, I learned the importance of copious research, balanced interpretation, and straightforward writing from my mentor and friend Professor Justus Doenecke of New College of Florida. *Il miglior fabbro.*

Most importantly, it is with endless love and boundless admiration that I thank Kathi Kapell. Not only did she live with this story's cast of cutthroat characters for far too long, but she did it with her inimitable grace. At every turn, she helped me transform Abe Reles's unusual story into a genuinely compelling one.

—Edmund Elmaleh, October 2008

About the Author

Edmund Elmaleh studied Murder, Inc., particularly the death of Abe Reles, for close to ten years. He held a degree in American History from New College of Florida, and was a member of the International Association of Crime Writers and the Organization of American Historians. He lived in Chicago until his death in 2008 as this book was being prepared for publication.